THE FOUR-WHEELER'S COMPANION

THE
FOUR-WHEELER'S
COMPANION

An Off-Road Guide to
Southwestern BC
THIRD EDITION

MARK BOSTWICK

HARBOUR PUBLISHING

Third edition copyright © 1995 by Mark Bostwick
Original edition published 1988

HARBOUR PUBLISHING CO. LTD.
Box 219, Madeira Park, BC Canada   V0N 2H0

Cover design by Roger Handling
Maps by Gaye Hammond
Photographs by the author except where noted
Printed and bound in Canada

CANADIAN CATALOGUING IN PUBLICATION DATA

Bostwick, Mark, 1939–
   The four-wheeler's companion

   ISBN 1-55017-118-6

   1. Trails—British Columbia—Guidebooks.
2. Automobiles—Four-wheel drive. 3. British
Columbia—Guidebooks. I. Title.
GV1025.C2B68 1995   917.11'3044   C94-910829-4

CONTENTS

ACKNOWLEDGEMENTS

This guidebook could not have been written without the help and encouragement of many others. Jud Barnes always had a new route up his sleeve. Sally Ann Terry, Jim Flack and Dennis Vrba were always willing to try it. Chester Ptasinski constantly ribbed me about my own eagerness to get on the road early. Robert Malanik provided a good winch and campfire philosophy until the embers began to fade. And Dave Joy was able to recall every adventure more vividly than real life. If you look closely you will see their rigs in the illustrations, along with all the Lionsgaters Four Wheel Drive Club who offered inspiration and support during the revision of this book.

This work is dedicated to Linda, Josh, Jeremy and four-wheelers everywhere.

INTRODUCTION

British Columbia may have the best four-wheeling in North America. Certainly the combination of great natural beauty and the constantly replenished legacy of abandoned roads provides us with an incredible abundance and variety of four-wheel drive challenges. The purpose of this guidebook is to share with the reader some of the many interesting four-wheel drive trails within a few hours' drive of Vancouver.

I have tried to provide a sampling of trails, both easy and difficult, that will appeal to the beginner and expert alike. Some of the routes detailed here are easy afternoon jaunts; others require considerable preparation and skill and should only be attempted by experienced drivers in a team.

Backroad travel is, by most studies, one of the most popular of all outdoor recreational activities. Thousands of vehicles are used simply to get away from the ordinary cares of daily life and into the backcountry. For many, the truck is a means to reach an inaccessible fishing hole, the base of a wilderness summit, a photogenic outlook or a secluded camping site. Others, when they are not fixing or modifying their trucks, enjoy four-wheeling for itself, or as a club activity with a group of friends. I fervently hope that all those who use four-wheel drive vehicles—including everything from the popular four-wheel drive cars to the big rigs outfitted with 33-inch tires and winches—will find something useful in the following pages.

Another purpose of this guide is to encourage responsible four-wheeling. Some sections of the public have the mistaken impression that four-wheeling is synonymous with destruction of the environment. This is partly a class bias because most four-wheelers are working people, and working people are usually presumed to be something they are not. Some critics of four-wheeling misread the term "off road" and assume it implies putting tire tracks across virgin wilderness. Nothing could be further from the truth; we four-wheelers follow existing, if often primitive, roads. Nor are we insensitive to the constant need to protect and extend our diminishing wilderness heritage. Virtually all four-wheelers are strong defenders of conservation. Lamentably, ownership of a four-wheel drive vehicle does not automatically confer responsibility, and a major goal of this guidebook is to preach, if you will, the virtues of care and respect for the outdoors.

Finally, this guidebook presumes to offer some advice and suggestions on how to increase your safety and enjoyment of recreational four-wheeling. Every experienced four-wheeler has strong opinions about which make or model of truck is best, what options and modifications are desirable. I have tried here to draw on the experience of others and to share it with you.

This volume is the result of several years' effort—attempting to jot down mileages while bumping across a flooded creek, orienting myself in a mountain fog, trying to keep up with drivers ahead while breathlessly making comments into a pocket tape recorder. Undoubtedly there are errors and omissions, and the author always stands ready to be corrected.

BC BACKROADS

The backcountry roads of British Columbia are rarely designed with any recreational use in mind; the sole reason for their existence is the efficient transport of ore and the hauling of logs. Thus, the pattern of logging roads usually consists of a main line fed by branches and spurs, all pointing to the mouth of the valley and the mills and markets beyond. Natural obstacles along the way are bridged, blasted, or circumvented. Main lines are wider and graded, for they are the most used, while branches and spurs become progressively rougher and more temporary. Since ridge lines tend to mark the boundaries of district forestry authority, few of our logging roads provide access to one valley from its opposite on the other side of the ridge. Mining roads built by prospectors are usually narrower, rougher and go as directly as possible to the location of a claim.

Logging roads, in particular, have become a source of controversy and the subject of elaborate new regulations. The provincial Forest Practices Code specifies the size of road cuts, the kind of road surfacing, and a series of required protections against erosion and toxic pollution. Bridges over creeks will no longer be hand crafted affairs constructed of four old growth logs and some rough planking spanning a stream in the most convenient way. Today they must be designed (often in concrete and steel) and certified by professional engineers, maintained on a regular basis until they are ditched, "de-activated" and finally dismantled. The process of dismantling will cut short the recreational potential of many backroads.

At the same time many older tracks and trails are now being re-activated to permit cutting of second growth. Older trails are ploughed under and replaced by large, wide roads capable of handing the most modern and insatiable heavy equipment.

HOW TO USE THIS BOOK

This guidebook uses a very traditional format. Each of the nine sections focusses on a recognizable starting point, e.g. Hope, Squamish, etc. I have tried to provide basic information on how to reach specific trailheads. A rating (for difficulty) precedes a detailed account of each route.

Unlike descriptions in a rock climber's guide or even in an ordinary backroad manual, the trail details are not always complete down to the last rock or muddy corner. After all, four-wheeling is exploring. Besides, few trails stay the same for very long. Next year's floods could easily wipe out a fragile bridge; last year's logging may have changed a road system. I have tried to indicate dead ends and danger spots, and, I hope, have reduced the possibility of uncomfortable surprises while retaining the chance to discover a flowery meadow or a challenging section of shelf road.

The four-wheeling season in this corner of British Columbia is normally mid-July to mid-October. There are plenty of places to go earlier in the year, and a few hardy souls venture into the woods even on winter weekends. If you find that some spots are drier than I suggested—or a lot muddier—do not be surprised. I probably did the trip in a different season.

All distance measurements in this book should be considered estimates. I have tried to be accurate, but when I

Deep water crossing

cut corners my mileages may be shorter; when I was lazy the cumulative total may be longer. And of course the amount of air in my tires—or in yours—can make a considerable difference. The same is true of the maps. They should be treated as suggestive sketches, not scientific surveys.

Travel books always bear a personal imprint, and many are positively idiosyncratic. This volume is no exception. My interest in four-wheeling grew out of an old mountain climber's desire to get to the foot of the high ridges without too much bushwhacking, consequently the clear preference here for roads to timberline. But four-wheeling, I soon discovered, was a sport unto itself, complete with special skills, legendary runs, and a unique comradeship.

This guidebook may be used by the solo adventurer, the man or woman who owns a 4 X 4 and takes off on Saturday to get away from it all. But I hope that most readers will look into the fun and adventure found through one of our province's many four-wheel drive clubs. This book owes a

Breakfast off the tailgate

special thanks to the members of the Lionsgaters Four Wheel Drive Club. There was no better way to learn the basics of four-wheeling than roughing it with others.

RATING SYSTEM

One man's meat is another man's poison. Keep in mind that all rating systems are arbitrary. The season, the weather, the vehicle, and the skill and mood of the driver will all have a day-to-day effect on the difficulty of a trip. The best a reader can hope for is a system that is as explicit as possible and relatively consistent. It follows that the way to use this rating system is to try a couple of trips and compare your experiences with mine, making your own adjustments for season, weather and mood on subsequent outings.

Class 1: Very easy. In effect a two-wheel drive backroad with virtually continuous driving over a smooth surface. Four-wheel drive cars should have no trouble. The probable use of "all four feet" is for compression coming downhill. Ordinary tires will be adequate.

Class 2: Easy. Continuous driving over rough surfaces with a few dips, bumps and sharp switchbacks. Pebbles, puddles and perhaps a bit of thin mud. Sometimes a few steep turns. Owners of small four-wheel drive cars may find themselves shifting into four-wheel drive for traction—or simply for a greater sense of security.

Class 3: Moderate. Often steep and sufficiently rough to cause some clearance problems for low-slung vehicles. Most drivers will find themselves pausing from time to time to decide how to approach a dip or streamlet, or how to squeeze their way through a narrow spot. Expect a high probability of a washed-out section, some downed timber, rocks on the road. Drivers of four-wheel drive cars will be pushing their luck. Others will be glad they have good shocks and let some air out of their tires.

Class 4: Moderately difficult. Continuous four-wheeling, mostly in high range but with a few sections where low range feels right. Obstacles will require stopping to check things out, move aside some boulders, clear away some trees, scrape out a bit of sidehill. Commonly a few axle-deep streams, badly washed-out sections, thick undergrowth. Since it is possible to get stuck, carry proper equipment and bring along energetic companions—or, even better, more than one vehicle.

Class 5: Difficult. Rugged terrain with all the joys of serious four-wheeling: deep water, mud holes, boulders, sharp rocks, shelf roads, deep ruts, low trees and a lot of stop-and-go driving. Count on using your shovel and be glad you remembered to bring a tow strap. Clearance is a real factor and novices will soon recognize that they have much to learn. Often a longer trail or one with a large altitude gain. Be fully equipped, don't go alone and plan on a long day.

Class 6: Difficult and perhaps dangerous to the vehicle. This is the realm of burnt clutches, dented skid plates, scratched fenders. Somebody will get stuck—although usually not seriously. Anticipate a point of no return and some route-finding problems—typically a pitch of ten or twenty yards that demands finesse as well as brute force. Carry extra fuel, extra food and a tool box. Don't go alone.

Class 7: Very difficult and dangerous. Usually a long trip with at least two full days of driving. Chances of doing some damage to the truck are better than 50/50. Even experienced drivers of well-outfitted vehicles will sweat. Typically there will be a really deep stream crossing, bogs, rockpiles or sandy sidehills. Somebody ought to have a winch. Never go alone.

Class 8: Very dangerous and difficult. The odds are against completing a trip like this, and wise four-wheelers will know when to call it a day. This is no place for a novice, and the team should be relatively small since the going will be slow. Most trucks will suffer some damage, and sometimes the sort of damage that requires a mechanic. Carry tools, parts, survival gear. Don't expect to be at work on Monday morning.

Class 9: Expeditionary driving. This kind of trip usually requires the approval of authorities, preparations for rescue, specialized equipment and advance planning. Class 9 trips are not covered in this guide.

Class 10: The impossible (until someone does it).

LEGEND

RIVER

PLACE NAME

BRIDGE

4WD TRAIL

HIGHWAY

SECONDARY TRAIL OR SIDEPATH

RAILWAY TRACK

MOUNTAIN

FOOTPATH

CAMPSITE

GATE

WASHOUT, BLOCKED ROAD

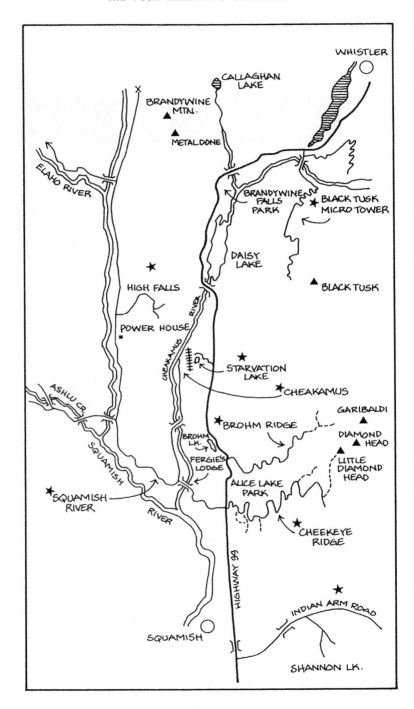

Section 1
SQUAMISH AREA

Off-roading between West Vancouver and Pemberton is like going fishing in the backyard. One is less likely to scare a black bear out of the bushes than to startle a couple of mountain bikers making love. The "Sea to Sky Highway" (Highway 99) snaking along Howe Sound, then past Squamish and Whistler, and finally over the hill into Pemberton is inexorably bringing the area into the orbit of the Lower Mainland. Squamish was once a port unconnected to the Lower Mainland, the exit point for the resources of the Interior. The British Columbia Railway (BCR) connection between Squamish and North Vancouver is as recent as 1956, a rugged road followed a couple of years later. Today the area is becoming a suburb of Vancouver. Hundreds of residents now commute from Squamish and Whistler to work in the city, and both towns, along with Pemberton, are growing rapidly. If timber, ore and shipping once formed the economic base of the region, today it is golf, condos and capuccino.

Despite the onslaught of development, there are a number of branch roads zigzagging up the mountain slopes to spectacular scenery. The Tantalus Range as seen from High Falls continues to live up to its name: seductive but untouchable ice and snow. Black Tusk broods over the valley like a dark figure guarding the wilderness beyond. The sandbars of the Indian River estuary are like a remote desert island.

It normally takes an hour to drive to Squamish, and another hour to reach Pemberton. This makes it possible to explore a trail, enjoy a picnic lunch, and be home before dinner. Those who wish to linger will find provincial campsites at Brohm Lake, Callaghan Lake, Alice Lake and Nairn Falls. Four-wheelers are reminded that this area is now shared by many recreationists and should, therefore, drive with discretion and consideration for others.

INDIAN ARM ROAD
Rating: 2

A mainline logging road starts just south of Squamish, swings past Stawamus Chief and Sky Pilot Mountain, and follows Indian River to the north end of Indian Arm. I always imagine myself following a back lane in order to take a peek at the Lower Mainland's rear yard. From the abandoned dock at the trail's end, one gets a good view of Indian Arm and the sailboats tacking as they head back to their berths in Deep Cove. Some weekends the traffic can be pretty heavy and the road dusty. At the same time, this might be a good place to get the feel of a new truck on a moderate and convenient trail.

The Indian Arm road is normally easy to find, although years ago an early four-wheeler started up the Stawamus River near nightfall in a dense Howe Sound fog. He bumped along in the darkness, taking a right turn up a narrow canyon lined with rock on both sides. After an hour in total darkness he came across two guys wearing carbide lamps. They looked at him quizzically and asked the driver if he was looking for the "way out." "I sure am," he replied. "Well,

The end of the road at Indian Arm

take the next left and follow for an hour and you'll be okay." Sixty minutes later he emerged, to his surprise, at Britannia Beach. It seems the Britannia mine shafts go all the way under Sky Pilot Mountain, and the four-wheeler had taken a wrong turn into one of the mineshafts.

GETTING THERE: Follow Highway 99 to the Stawamus Chief, past the parking area, and go down the hill to the bridge over the Stawamus River. The road starts just south of the bridge. Turn right.

DESCRIPTION: Head up the road, passing a road that joins from the left at 2.7 km, and the woodlot sign at 3.1 km. At 3.4 km pass a house and stay right on the Stawamus Forest Road. Pass a gated road on the left at 3.8 km.

Cross a bridge at 4.5 km and note the view of the stream, and start uphill. If you are an inexperienced four-wheeler this might be a good place to lock into 4WD. At 4.9 km come to a fork. The right fork heads the ridges above

Shannon Falls (see below), the left fork is the Indian River road.

At 5.6 km you will catch a glimpse of Sky Pilot Mountain. At 6.6 km cross a bridge and join the powerline. The road begins to level out at 7.5 km, crosses a rockslide at 8.7 km. It is necessary to cross a number of shallow ditches in this section.

Stay left at 12 km, and join the stream on the left at 13 km. At 14.5 km the road crosses to the other side of the valley and starts uphill. We forded two small streams in the next section before dropping down to the valley at 20.5 km. Stay right at 21 km. Indian River comes into view around 23 km. There are side roads to small campsites in this section.

The road crosses the river on two bridges at 30 km. There are several campsites in this area. At 32 km a road to the left heads for Norton Lake; stay straight for Indian Arm. Pass through the old logging camp at 34 km, and follow the scent of salt water to the upper end of Indian Arm at 36 km.

 NORTON LAKE
Rating: 5

Many travellers along the Indian River Road like to make a side trip to Norton Lake. The trail is old and wearing out, which provides much of its appeal to those four-wheelers who like rock crawling, dense bush, and the reward of a cold alpine lake ringed with bleached white logs. On my last trip I noticed markings on the trees that suggest that this road may be "improved" (sic) in the near future.

GETTING THERE: Follow the directions for the Indian Arm road to the point (32 km) just after the two bridges, and take the side road to the left (0 km).

DESCRIPTION: The trail starts uphill on a bed of pebbles, then crosses a beautiful deep canyon at .6 km. After crossing the bridge, the road switchbacks uphill through the forest.

At 2.3 km there is a major intersection. Stay left. Watch out for the sharp corner with a dip at 3.5 km, and go slow and easy on the rocks. The bush begins to close in, knocking your rearview mirrors back during this section.

At 5.8 km stay right. At 6.4 km stay left. Rock crawling. Stay left again at 6.6 km. At 7.1 km the roads left and right both lead to the lake. The lake, the wind, and usually mosquitoes are found at 7.4 km.

SHANNON CREEK
Rating: 1–2

The Shannon Creek road climbs to some satisfying views down Howe Sound, yet it is short enough to be done on a Sunday afternoon after church. The trail circles around behind Stawamus Chief and then winds up the slopes above Shannon Falls to an altitude of about 1000 meters.

GETTING THERE: Drive north along the Sea to Sky Highway past the pull-off beneath the Chief, continue down the hill towards Squamish but do not cross the bridge at the bottom. Instead, turn right onto the logging road (0 km).

DESCRIPTION: Follow the road uphill for 3 km, crossing a bridge and staying right. At 3.4 km stay right at the fork past the house.

At 4.9 km come to another fork, this one with Forest Service signs. Go right up the Stawamus/Shannon Forest Road.

Stay right at 5.2 km. The road begins to climb, zigzagging upward as it rounds the hill. By the time you reach 9.5 km the view becomes spectacular.

At 11 km the road levels off a little, and at 11.2 km stay left, crossing a bridge at 12.7. Enjoy another alpine vista. At 14.3 stay right, and at 14.5 stay right again. More viewpoints. The road ends at 16.7 km.

SQUAMISH RIVER—ELAHO—ASHLU
Rating: 1

For those whose geography is a little fuzzy, the Squamish River does not flow from Pemberton to Squamish. Rather, it is a subsidiary of the Cheakamus, flowing from the north to a confluence just north of Brackendale.

Its interest to four-wheelers is perhaps less than its interest to other recreationists: fishing and picnicking along the riverbanks, hiking up the mountainsides, and perhaps kayaking in the river. The scenery, however, on a clear day (and this is not common since great icefields behind the valley encourage a steady supply of clouds) can be stunning. The main road up the Squamish is fairly well maintained, if a bit bumpy, but is also the main route out for dozens of logging trucks, travelling any day of the week. Drivers are cautioned to take particular care along this road.

GETTING THERE: Drive north from the Squamish stoplight for 9.1 km, and turn left towards Cheekeye. Follow

The Elaho River (Keith Thirkell photo)

the road past the dump, the airport, a power station, over the railway tracks and across the Cheakamus River, and turn left.

DESCRIPTION: The main line is the Squamish River Road. From the intersection beyond the bridge (0 km), follow the pavement through several settlements (watch for kids and livestock), past the Weldwood Logging Company gatehouse at 19.1 km (usually open, sometimes staffed), and onto mostly gravel road. The Ashlu branch takes off left at approximately 22.3 km, while straight ahead you will pass the Cheakamus powerhouse (speed bumps on a short paved stretch) which brings water down the mountainside to the right.

The road follows the Squamish River, passing a variety of riverbank picnic sites and the Elaho turn-off (to the left) at 44.0 km. This is now an active logging area, and the road becomes rougher, angling up the side of the mountain. Stay left at 55.0 km through the slash. (A side road to the left, dropping down to a bridge across the river, ends upriver

Elaho—four-wheeling in the snow, early spring

not far from the crossing.) Meanwhile, your progress on the main road may be halted a few kilometres later by the deterioration of a bridge over a stream that flows off the shoulders of Ring Mountain to the right. If this obstacle can be passed, the road may continue for another 10 or 15 km towards the headwaters.

A glance at the map shows that the headwaters of the Squamish are tantalizingly close to the headwaters of the Soo River Valley; perhaps someday a circle route, up the Squamish and down the Soo to the Cheakamus, might be possible.

Ashlu Creek: The turn-off (to the left) is 22.3 km from the Cheakamus Bridge. This road crosses the creek once again 2.0 km farther on, and then again a couple of kilometres farther on before following the Ashlu Creek on the right. The area has been extensively logged in the lower reaches and a new road also crosses the creek to the south to more logging and an active mine. The various spur roads on this south branch lead nowhere, although there are optimists who believe one of them makes a fabled link with the roads behind Port Mellon. Realists will forego these diversions and continue up the Ashlu until they are halted by logging. As recently as 1989, it was possible to follow the Ashlu for well over 20 km.

Elaho River: This is the most attractive of the three branches of the Squamish River Valley. It extends for approximately 30 km from the turn-off at 44.0 km. Along the way, the road passes impressive views of the gorge (2.0 km beyond the turn-off, and again by Maude Frickert Creek at 7.0 km) as it winds around the mountainsides to the north of the Elaho. Beyond 7.0 km the road returns to the valley, with a variety of side roads leading down to sandbars and riverbanks on the left. Undoubtedly, the road system will someday extend to the headwaters of the Elaho (close to the head of the Pemberton Valley) and to those of another subsidiary, the Clenndenning, which is fed by glaciers and is not too far from the streams feeding Toba Inlet.

Of the three choices, the Elaho is the longest and also the nicest for picnics and scenery. It is also the home of a highly protected herd of moose.

 ## HIGH FALLS
Rating: 1

This logging road climbs out of the Squamish valley along the shoulders of High Falls Creek. The creek drains an alpine basin beneath Tricouni Peak, a popular destination of summer hikers and spring skiers who use the road to reach a starting point not far from timberline. The falls themselves are some distance away across the valley, and they are no Niagara, but the views to the southwest, across the Squamish River to the Tantalus Range, are impressive.

GETTING THERE: Drive north out of Squamish and turn left at Cheekeye, passing the airport and power station to Fergie's Lodge on the Cheakamus. Cross the bridge and stay left to enter the Squamish River Valley. Continue along this road through the Weldwood gate and past the power station. Approximately 1.5 km past the power station, turn off onto a logging road on the right.

DESCRIPTION: The first section of road is a little rough, but after a couple of corners the road enters the shelter of the forest and remains in excellent condition.

The road climbs to the shoulder (approximately 4.0 km) and follows it towards the high country. High Falls is visible below and to the east. The road ends at an old log dump site at 8.0 km. Hikers and skiers start here and head towards the stream and then traverse north towards timberline.

CHEAKAMUS RIVER ROAD
Rating: 1

The Cheakamus River Road is more for picnicking than four-wheeling. Historically this was the road to Starvation Lake, but that has been stopped. Before that, adventurers would ford the Cheakamus River and follow an old skidder road up the other side, but that too is blocked. And so the Cheakamus River Road is now a place for a picnic.

GETTING THERE: From Squamish, drive north on Highway 99 to the big intersection for Cheekeye (right) and Paradise Valley (left). Turn left and follow the road past the dump and the transformers to the Cheakamus River at Fergie's Lodge.

DESCRIPTION: From Fergie's Lodge cross the bridge and turn right and head north. Pass the Outdoor School turnoff at 2.1 km, cross the bridge at 3 km. At 4.1 km cross the railway tracks and stay left on McNaught Way. At 5.1 km cross the railway tracks again and stay right. Stay right at the Jack Webster bridge. The gravel road gets a little rougher from here until it ends at 11.1 km. There is room for a couple of trucks, a boulder-covered riverbank and a sense of seclusion.

The trail appears to continue uphill, but quickly reaches a dead end a few hundred yards farther on, where the BCR has obliterated the trail with boulders. You may wish to hike into Starvation Lake which is a few thousand metres uphill on the other side of the tracks.

BROHM RIDGE
Rating: 3–6

Take this short side trip on a bright, sunny Sunday morning and enjoy the scenery. The Brohm Ridge trail was intended as the access road for a ski area that was abandoned halfway through construction. Now it is a snowmobile trail.

Mist on Brohm Ridge

Brohm Ridge by night (Keith Thirkell photo)

The foundations of the old ski tow mid-station provide an excellent place to stop and look down on Howe Sound, and beyond it to the faint edge of snow on the Olympic Peninsula. On the other side of the valley, the rocky shoulders of the Tantalus Range are draped in snow and ice; here and there waterfalls plummet through hemlock forests. And to the east, especially in May or June, the flanks of Garibaldi are still sheathed in ice. Often the sounds of avalanches and rockfalls reverberate across the valley.

GETTING THERE: Drive north on Highway 99 past Squamish and past Alice Lake Park. Continue on the highway for 3.5 km to a left curve (a few hundred metres south of Brohm Lake), and watch for a logging road that drops to the right off the highway (0 km).

DESCRIPTION: Take the logging road (level ground) and follow it, crossing under the power lines and over Brohm Creek (0.2 km) and then angling right and uphill. Ignore the side road to the left and approach a junction. Stay right and go through the gate at 1.6 km. Pass the turn-off to the Cat Lake campground and continue to the power line at 2.4 km.

The trail now zigzags uphill towards the ridge with a few worn places that are generally passable, although a little narrow in spots. Eventually the trail levels off at the old mid-station foundations. This is a good place to pause for a glance back towards Howe Sound.

After a wet winter there is often snow drifted into the curves on the next section, but late in the summer it is usually possible to continue over a shoulder and then down to a meadow leading up to the snowmobile club chalets (13.0 km). On a clear day the view of Garibaldi is spectacular.

Four-wheeler Russell Whieldon has taken his truck for several kilometres beyond this point and reports that the track winds along the ridge. He successfully negotiated an old slide area, although he recommends "extreme caution," and continued to a steep incline that is cut by a runoff gully. Beyond this the road forks, with one fork heading west and the other east. Again, late snow is likely to make this section impassable in all but the dryest years.

STARVATION LAKE
Rating: 7

Old timers think this secluded spot aptly named. Once there were three ways into the lake, today barely one. Originally, four-wheelers drove to a scenic picnic area along Highway 99, and dropped down along a rickety little shelf road above the BCR tracks. First the Highways Department put up concrete barriers, and only mountain bikers could get down the road. More recently, the BCR has sheared off the cliff and eliminated a large section of the old trail. The BCR also dumped boulders over the second approach, which led uphill from the Cheakamus River to the lake. The remaining route includes a steep, very rugged downhill section. More than a few trucks have reached the lake, but had to call a tow truck to get back out again. The lake itself is small and shrouded in a cloud of starving mosquitoes.

GETTING THERE: Drive from Squamish past the Alice Lake turn-off and Brohm Lake. Approximately 13 km from the Alice Lake turn-off, there is an old roadhouse site on the right which is currently being developed. The Starvation Lake road takes off left just before this site.

DESCRIPTION: The track winds through the forest for a little over a kilometre and comes to a small promontory before curving right and traversing the slope down to the lake. Do not head down until you have reconnoitered, for the only turn-around is at the bottom. The track is steep and has been washed down to bare rock. Even experienced drivers with powerful trucks and good tires may have difficulty coming back up again.

The lake is at the bottom of this hill. The road around

the lake used to lead out to the Cheakamus River, but is now solidly blocked where it crosses the railway tracks. The trail leading right once went back up to the highway, but it has also been purposely destroyed. However, enough of the trail may remain to give hikers a view of the trains snaking down the Cheakamus canyon.

CHEEKEYE RIDGE
Rating: 2

This is a short, steep climb to super views and the start of a pleasant hike through alpine country for very little effort. For those who want to take a closer look at the four summits (Dalton Dome, Mount Garibaldi, Atwell Peak and Little Diamond Head), which valley pounders abbreviate to "Garibaldi," this is an ideal trip. Take water, mosquito repellent and a flower book, and watch out for black bears.

GETTING THERE: Drive north on Highway 99 past Squamish to the Alice Lake Park entrance, and turn into the park.

DESCRIPTION: Take the paved left fork at the entrance (0 km), and then go right onto a potholed dirt road, which heads back towards Edith Lake. Before the lake, take a left fork, and follow the road through the brush to a series of switchbacks that ascend the ridge for 6.5 km (and 1200 metres altitude gain) to another major fork on the north side of the ridge.

The left branch will take you to a pile of slash, the starting point for hikers heading up Little Diamond Head. The right fork crosses the ridge to the south slopes and ends a few hundred metres below the ridge line.

If you take the right branch and still wish to hike, don't drive all the way to the end of the logging road. Stop at a point where the ridge looks lowest. Get out your hiking boots and climb to the ridge (a little bushwhacking followed by sub-alpine meadows), then hike along it to a picnic spot and viewpoint of the summits.

This abandoned logging road presents no difficulties except for a few dips in the road and the occasional loose rock. It takes no more than an hour to trundle up from Alice Lake Park to the end of the road, and another hour on foot to the best views of the mountain.

BLACK TUSK MICROWAVE TOWER
Rating: 1–2

As one drives along Highway 99 past Daisy Lake, the Black Tusk microwave tower is prominently displayed on the ridge to the west, not far from the impressive black volcanic core of Black Tusk. The access road, as can be plainly seen from the highway, collects a great deal of snow and is often not driveable on its upper reaches until late in the season. For this reason, the road is popular with summer skiers.

Black Tusk microwave tower

GETTING THERE: Once again, take Highway 99 past the "Welcome to Whistler" sign, and turn right at Function Junction across the road from the Whistler Service Park (0 km).

DESCRIPTION: Instead of turning left by the dredge, stay on the main road, but avoid the dump by going left at the fork.

Follow the dirt road up the valley for 5.1 km to a BC Hydro sign—which conveniently informs you that the trail to the right is a four-wheel drive route. Not a difficult one, however; just steep switchbacks that seem to double back on top of one another, levelling out to pass through a strange, dead forest and across a rocky bridge, before ascending once more by switchbacks to the crest of the ridge at 12.0 km. Late snow may stop you at this point.

If you can continue, the country opens up, as you have gained over 1800 metres and are approaching timberline. The track, which is now rocky, approaches a dip in the ridge just below the tower. This is a good place to stop, because the views in any direction are superb: to the east the snowy peaks of Garibaldi Park; to the west the Tantalus Range; and, of course, the shaded black face of the tusk dominates the south.

Protecting the fragile alpine grasses and flowers is a responsibility of four-wheelers: stay on the trail and do your exploring on foot. From the microwave tower it is an hour's hike over snowfields and tundra to a grand viewpoint overlooking Taylor Meadows and Garibaldi Lake.

COUGAR MOUNTAIN FOREST ROAD
Rating: 1–2

This short side trip is popular with mountain bikers and hikers from Whistler, and is perhaps best done during the late autumn, before the snowfall.

GETTING THERE: Follow Highway 99 through the municipality of Whistler and watch for the Cougar Mountain sign a short distance beyond the north end of Green Lake. Turn west onto the road.

DESCRIPTION: Follow the track as it winds uphill, staying left at the signposted junction and passing a small lake on the right. A brief steep section brings you to a log dump at 6.7 km, and a number of short dead-end spur roads. I was able to get a few glimpses of the Soo River valley before the October mist closed in.

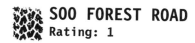 ## SOO FOREST ROAD
Rating: 1

The Soo River meanders down a broad swampy valley and joins with the north-flowing Green River. This active logging road seems to have no significant recreational use and is perhaps best described as the kind of place to visit when you do not seek exertion but only the chance to feast your eyes on the russets and golds of autumn foliage.

GETTING THERE: Drive past Whistler and its condo suburbs for approximately 3 km. Watch for the Soo Forest Road sign on your left just before Highway 99 crosses the BCR tracks at Green River.

DESCRIPTION: The good road skirts the flanks of Cougar Mountain on the left, passes signs at 3.0 km and crosses a bridge at 3.5 km. The valley broadens at 8.0 km.

At 11.0 km, there is a fork. The right fork switchbacks up to an active logging site on the mountainside. I stayed straight along the valley floor. At 17.0 km I took the right fork and started uphill, hoping to reach some clearing or trailhead to the surrounding ridges. Alas, the logging road came to an abrupt end at 19.0 km. I retreated to the meadows for lunch.

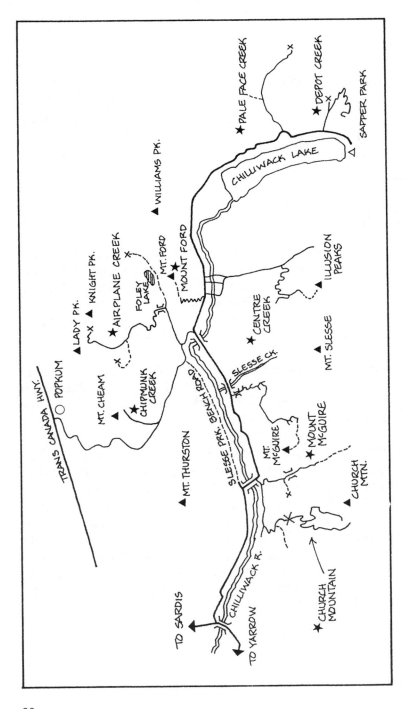

Section 2

CHILLIWACK RIVER VALLEY

The Chilliwack River Valley has few rivals as an outdoor recreation area. On any given summer weekend, one is likely to see river rafting, slalom kayaking, scores of fishermen, canoeists on the lake, hikers plodding up the trails and not a few climbers striking out for the high ridges. The main road along the river valley from Vedder Crossing runs for 53.0 km before reaching the south end of Chilliwack Lake, just north of the US border. Subsidiary valleys joining the main valley on either side greatly extend the recreational potential. Almost all the high ridge lines are accessible to the average hiker—and the reward is an unparalleled alpine view, including majestic Mount Baker.

Most of the old logging roads are still open, and although the four-wheeling is only moderately difficult, the attraction of getting beyond the trees is compelling. This is also historic country. Several of the passes were used by Indians and later by traders coming from the south and heading for the gold fields.

There are several organized campgrounds: Chilliwack River, towards the mouth, Foley Lake, and Sapper Creek at the south end of Chilliwack Lake. Smaller campsites dot both sides of the river. Best of all, the road is partly paved, thus sparing the four-wheeler the usual jolting drive along a potholed road just to get to the head of a four-wheel drive trail.

To reach the Chilliwack River Valley, drive east on Highway 1 to the Chilliwack/Cultus Lake exit (No. 3 Road), then south through Yarrow (turn into town just past the Majuba Casket Company), and along the base of the hills to the bridge and intersection. Cross the bridge and go right, immediately entering the Chilliwack River Valley.

The river road is well maintained for most of the way. Just before the first bridge (which crosses to the south side of the river), at Slesse Park, there is a fork to the left; this road follows the north bank all the way to Foley Lake. It is a diversion, but also very potholed.

After crossing to the south side, the main road passes a number of forestry camps and correctional facilities, and another major bridge over Slesse Creek. Next comes a bridge across the Chilliwack, and a turn-off (left) to Foley Lake and the Bench Road and several trailheads mentioned below.

The surface on the main road becomes quite a bit rougher towards Chilliwack Lake, and some of the corners on the road around the lake are blind. The road ends at the Sapper campground, where many launch their canoes.

All in all, the Chilliwack River Valley is a delightful area—a place to treat with respect, because it will be impossible to find a more accessible area for four-wheeling so close to Vancouver.

 ## CHURCH MOUNTAIN
Rating: 3
Altitude Gain: 1600 metres

The peaks above Cultus Lake are connected by a bewildering tangle of old and new logging roads. The Little Tamihi

Creek Road is connected to several other networks of logging roads, but is here kept relatively separate since it does lead to an objective: a short, calf-stretching hike to the summit (and views) of Church Mountain.

This is an active logging area, which means two things: be careful, and expect some mud holes and ruts, especially early in the season. The difficulty of the route will depend upon the season and the amount of logging; many four-wheel drive cars (as opposed to trucks) will probably be able to get high enough to sample the views and shorten the walk to the ridge.

GETTING THERE: Drive from the mouth of the Chilliwack River Valley at Vedder Crossing to the first bridge (just beyond the Slesse Park fork). After stopping to check out the kayak slalom course, cross the bridge and turn right down a gravel road.

DESCRIPTION: After crossing the bridge (0 km) and turning right, drive for 2.3 km, crossing two streams, and take a road coming in from your left.

Follow this road uphill into the second growth forest, staying right at 3.9 km and passing the Forest Road sign. At 4.7 km there is another branch. Stay left this time. (The right branch angles around into another watershed and another ridge—see below).

The trail now meanders upward through the trees, a cool leafy tunnel in mid-summer, past an active logging site at 5.1 km and then back into the trees at 6.0 km. In the winter of 1990, unfortunately, an avalanche swept across this section of road, depositing a large amount of logs, forest debris and rock. It looks, however, as if a determined group might clear this section and proceed up the mountain.

There is a switchback at 6.6 km, and at 8.3 km a road enters sharply from the right. If you do not turn, but continue straight on, the trail eventually crosses the creek, climbs around a little knob (good view from the other side), and comes back into the main valley before climbing to an active logging site below the east ridge of Church Mountain.

If you turn right and uphill at 8.3 km, the road will take you higher (although it comes within fifty feet of the other branch higher up the bowl) via two long switchbacks. At 13.1 km you will reach the crest of the ridge (with a view of Liumchen Mountain and the Chilliwack Valley smog), and will then traverse the side slope back towards Church Mountain. The trail ends at a log sorting clearing at 13.9 km.

It is a thirty-minute scramble through the greenery to the ridge, and another thirty or forty minutes along the ridge to the open summit of Church Mountain. The view from the summit includes Mount Baker, Mount Tomyhoi and all the peaks along the Chilliwack River.

Note: If you go right at 4.7 km, the road heads towards Cultus Lake. Approximately 3.9 km along this road there is a left branch, which will take you up another ridge. Stay left at one fork. We were stopped by snow after 6.0 km, but it looks like this trail leads across a bowl to a ridge west of the one described above.

MOUNT McGUIRE ROAD
Rating: 3

We four-wheelers co-exist with logging, and sometimes it seems like our passage through a devastated forest is a high price to pay for a good run or a great view. The logging on the flanks of Slesse and Borden Creeks is not pretty, but the easy hike to the top of Mount McGuire is beautiful. The logging in this area is extensive, but the right combination of forks ends up at a hiking trail leading up a narrow ridge to the top of Mount McGuire.

GETTING THERE: Enter the Chilliwack Valley at Vedder Crossing and follow the road for 19.8 km to a turn-off immediately before the Slesse Creek bridge (the second major bridge in the valley).

DESCRIPTION: A few hundred yards beyond the turn-off (0 km), the road is blocked by a closed gate in front of a bridge. The gate is open during the week, and a watchman is usually there until 6:30 p.m. on weekends.

After crossing the bridge, take the right fork. At 4.7 km stay right again.

At 8.8 km stay left.

At 10.3 km stay right. These forks take you away from Slesse Creek and around the side of the mountain to the Borden Creek watershed. There are a few steep spots and probably some stray rocks on the road, but nothing to get worried about.

As the road reaches the head of a small bowl, there are three branches. The left branch will take you closest to a tape-marked trail (orange tape wrapped around a tree trunk) at 13.9 km.

The hiking trail zigzags through the forest to the foot of a steep, narrow ridge. A bit of scrambling will get you to the summit from the truck in about an hour.

CENTRE CREEK
Rating: 3–4

The farther one drives up the Chilliwack River Valley, the higher and more rugged are the mountains on either side. The great snaggletooth of Mount Slesse, the imposing sugarloaf of Williams Peak, the gigantic lap of snow on Tomyhoi Peak, and Canadian Border Peak, which looks like the gods gave it a tweak and twisted its summit, rival the shimmering dome of Mount Baker. The Centre Creek Road allows one to get reasonably close to high altitude, high-angle climbing in the region. If you are not a climber, but a photographer or an explorer, the views will be just as inspirational.

There are several spurs and side roads off the main Centre Creek road. The one that gives the best views—and reaches within a few hundred metres of a ridge leading to the sheer slabs of Illusion Peak—is at 4.4 km.

GETTING THERE: After entering the valley, cross the first bridge (kayak slalom course), the second bridge (over Slesse Creek), and the third bridge (over the Chilliwack River). Watch for the Riverside Campsite, approximately 5 km from the third bridge, and turn right, crossing the Chilliwack once again to the south side.

DESCRIPTION: After crossing the Chilliwack River, go left along the river, crossing Centre Creek and turning right onto the marked logging road.

The trail is usually in good shape, although scattered with rocks, especially in the narrower sections. The main line follows the bottom of the valley to its head, with branches on the left snaking up the flanks of Mounts Lindeman and MacDonald.

Towards the head of the valley the road becomes much rougher, especially near the huge landslide that pulled away a good part of the mountainside after clearcutting.

At 4.4 km from the start of the trail, a fork to the right

Crossing a small stream near Centre Creek

crosses the creek and meanders up the slopes of Illusion Peak for another five kilometres. From this point it is a forty-five minute bushwhack to the ridge leading towards the summit. There are spectacular views, but reaching the summit of Illusion Peak requires ropes and other alpine equipment.

MOUNT FORD LOOKOUT
Rating: 4

I always supposed this road, shown on the maps as climbing to the ridge and looping around the summit of Mount Ford, led to a working fire lookout. Not true. The road makes seventeen switchbacks and ends in a clearing on the ridge a kilometre or two from the foundations of what was once a fire lookout. The road is consequently deteriorating, although the marked hiking trail from the end of the road to the summit receives an annual clearing by a local hiking group.

Camping above Centre Creek valley

GETTING THERE: The trailhead is 2.1 km past the third bridge (where the gravel road crosses back to the north side of the river) in the Chilliwack River Valley, and is a sharp left.

DESCRIPTION: Once you are on track it is hard to get lost, since there are no branches, just switchbacks. You may be halted by fallen trees. In several places the surface has been washed away to bare rock. The trip ends in a clearing with orange tape markers indicating the footpath to the summit on the right.

PALEFACE CREEK
Rating: 1

The easy, leisurely, Paleface Creek logging road approaches, but does not cross, the historic Whatcom Trail Pass, which was temporarily a major pack trail from the USA into the BC interior. Now it is an example of the destruction caused by forest fires; the sides of several mountains are prickled with burnt matchsticks.

A branch of the Paleface Creek Road climbs a narrow valley behind Mount Meronuik but, regrettably, does not cross the divide into Upper Silverhope Creek. If it did, it would permit four-wheelers to make an interesting connection from the Chilliwack River Valley to the Skagit Valley.

GETTING THERE: Drive the length of the Chilliwack River Valley to the road along the lake shore. At approximately 47.0 km from Vedder Crossing, the road jogs inland and then turns back towards the lake near the Catermole Timber Co. shack. The road up Paleface Creek starts right behind the shack (0 km).

DESCRIPTION: This road follows the valley floor and is not difficult. It runs for about 10 to 12 km to a bushy area not far from the scree and talus slopes of the headwall.

A north branch (left), about 2.7 km up the valley from

the Catermole shack, goes for about 2 or 3 km. It is a bit worn and rough (Class 4), and splits into several spurs near the headwaters of the nameless creek. The left spur reaches to within a few hundred feet of the divide that separates the Chilliwack River Valley from the Skagit.

As one drives up the main valley, the road crosses several streams, two of which provide nearly perfect skinny-dipping and sunbathing opportunities.

DEPOT CREEK
Rating: 1–2

In case the road up Depot Creek is overgrown, the alternative is to climb a mountainside on the south side of the valley that almost, but not quite, provides an overview of Chilliwack Lake. From the switchbacks it is easy to spot the cut in the forest, made by the US to mark the border.

GETTING THERE: Drive to Chilliwack Lake, nearly to the end (approximately 50.5 km), where the road swings east. Just before a bridge, a well-worn road takes off to the left and up the Depot Creek Valley (0 km).

DESCRIPTION: The road is overgrown on both sides, and is eventually blocked at 3.0 km, but a branch to the right crosses the valley and ascends the slope. The road is clearly visible as it switchbacks up the mountain, heading for a bump to the west, overlooking the lake. There are a few small, seasonal watercourses to cross, and in places the road is rather rough. From the end—about 8.0 km from the turn-off—it is a quick hike to get a view down on Chilliwack Lake.

AIRPLANE CREEK
Rating: 6
Altitude Gain: 1000 metres

The Airplane Creek logging road takes only an hour to drive. It climbs steadily to a cleared area not far below the ridge systems leading from, and connecting to, Lady and Knight peaks. Once again the alpine scenery is delicious, and the photographer may concentrate on vast skylines or tiny alpine flowers.

Foley Lake, just up the forest road from the Airplane Creek turn-off, is an emerald set among the trees. There is a small campsite at the west end and trails taking off in several directions. The old logging road beyond the lake, however, is blocked a few kilometres farther on by a huge washout.

GETTING THERE: Drive up the Chilliwack River Valley for about 25.5 km, or just past the third bridge, which takes you to the north side of the river. (Old roads on the downstream side are now washed out.) Turn left almost immediately after crossing the bridge, and follow the road to an intersection. The road to the right is the Foley Lake Forest Road, which leads to the Airplane Creek turn-off and then to Foley Lake; the left turn goes down the valley past the Chipmunk Creek turn-off and eventually to Slesse Park. The road tends to be bumpy and nearly washed out as it follows the creek towards Foley Lake.

DESCRIPTION: Once you turn right onto the Foley Lake Forest Road (0 km), follow it for 1.5 km, crossing a stream. Look for a left branch that crosses a good bridge and heads steeply uphill. This is the road up Airplane Creek.

The road has been abandoned by loggers and has become quite rough. After switchbacking to gain altitude, the road follows the west flank of the mountainside. The small ditches cut to drain the water off the road are easily passable, but the bare rock washouts are a challenge. This deterioration has advanced the difficulty of this trip tremendously, and in the foreseeable future the whole road may be washed away.

At 9.6 km take the right branch, which follows the valley, and about 2.0 km farther on take the fork that will lead you farthest uphill, to the logged patch beneath the ridge. From this patch it is a twenty-minute scramble to the ridge. To the east is a ridge connecting Lady Peak with Knight Peak, both of which are part of the range including Welch and Foley peaks.

Note: The left fork at 9.6 km angles up the mountain and onto a timberline shoulder with fine views of Illusion Peak and Slesse. Some rockfall litters the road, but you can usually get around it. If the main road is blocked by snow-fed streamlets in the early summer, this is an alternative conclusion to the trip.

CHIPMUNK–POPKUM TRAVERSE
Rating: 2

This route may be done from either Popkum on the Trans-Canada Highway, or from the Chilliwack River Valley and Chipmunk Creek. The Chipmunk Creek approach is the more spectacular, because at the top one is suddenly treated to an expansive view of the Fraser Valley, and then a brief bit of vertigo as one follows a shelf road down to civilization. There are side roads on both sides which provide access to Mount Cheam, although the one on the Chipmunk side is by far the easier. The north side of the mountain retains snowbanks till mid-summer, so this trip is often best in the late summer or early fall.

GETTING THERE: Follow the Chilliwack River Valley Road from Vedder Crossing for approximately 26 km, past the third bridge (bringing you back to the north side of the river), and hang a left.

Follow this offshoot to the Foley Lake intersection, turn left down the Forest Road and cross two bridges, the second of which is Chipmunk Creek. Take the fork to the right and up the Chipmunk Creek Forest Service Road (0 km).

DESCRIPTION: Starting at this fork (0 km), drive up a steep but smooth road, following the mountain slopes through heavily logged areas.

At 4.6 km a road forks right. This road drops down, then climbs again to an old log dump, and parking for those who wish to climb Mount Cheam. It is a short (less than one hour) hike through alpine meadows and along a narrow ridge to the summit.

The left fork continues upward and traverses the ridge

Chipmunk–Popkum Traverse—the pass

to a small pass. The view from the pass is quite remarkable. On the other side of the pass the road is relatively narrow, and drops down the mountainside in a series of switchbacks. A side road to the right will take you back up the hill and to a basin below the Cheam Ridge.

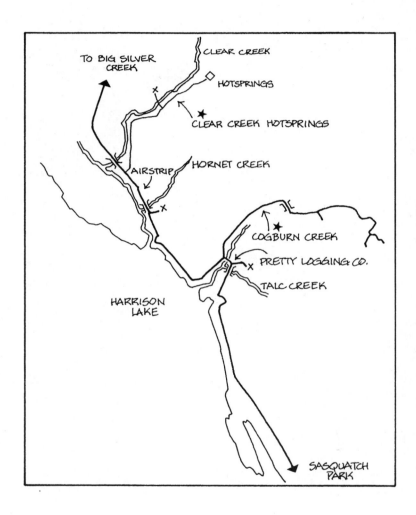

Section 3
HARRISON LAKE AREA

The two large lakes, Lillooet and Harrison, that slant down from Pemberton to Harrison Hot Springs resort and the Fraser River, have long been a pathway for travelers. The first trails were blazed by Indians, apparently to reach the prime fishing grounds. During the gold rush of the last century, steamboats sailed this freshwater inland sea, while indentured labourers hacked rough tracks through the forest.

Next came the loggers. The great stands of timber, which had once been an impediment to travel, now became a major source of profit. Presumably the oldest roads in this area, which has dozens of logging branches and spurs, have been overgrown for generations. The more recent tracks await the exploration of four-wheelers.

The latest phase of development is symbolized by Harrison Hot Springs, a resort town with hotels, motels, ice cream parlours, windsurfing, fishing and picnic lunches. Interspersed with the weekend stream of traffic arriving from Highway 1 (south bank of Fraser River) and Highway 7 (north bank of Fraser River) are always some four-wheelers.

This is also the reputed home of the legendary Sasquatch, a humanoid beast who roams the hills and occasionally darts across the road through the ever-present dust. Of the several theories about the origins of the Sasquatch, the most plausible is that he is an early four-wheeler who failed to carry a spare and got a flat up Harrison Lake. Ingeniously, he took out his round, dust-clogged air filter and soaked it in the lake, leaving it to dry overnight. In the morning he found the filter had hardened into mud, and he was able to bolt it on as a temporary spare tire. The air filter was not as big as his regular wheel, though, so he kept going round and round in circles until he went mad and ran off into the bushes.

The two main starting points for four-wheeling in the area are: Harrison Mills, specifically the Sasquatch Inn, on Highway 7 past Dewdney; and Harrison Hot Springs resort, which is reached by turning off Highway 1 and following Highway 9 through Agassiz.

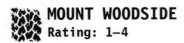 MOUNT WOODSIDE
Rating: 1–4

Many four-wheelers scan maps with a magnifying glass in hopes of finding obscure through-routes, which start one place and end another. All too many of our old roads follow a valley or ridge to a headwall and then simply end. Mount Woodside looked like it might be an exception. I was wrong.

Mount Woodside, that large, shaggy lump that sits southwest of Harrison Hot Springs, may be climbed to its long summit ridge, but the road does not continue down the other side (as shown on some maps). An overgrown track does start down, but it peters out at the last power pylon.

Just to make sure, we searched for a way up from the valley floor. Once, long ago, there may have been a skid road down the mountainside, but a farmer's ditch and a completely overgrown stream have obliterated all possible hopes.

On the other hand, a tour of Mount Woodside provides views of the Fraser Valley, the outlet of Harrison Lake, and mountain ranges in almost all directions. The small lakes on the ridge are full of fish.

The road becomes progressively rougher, but four-wheel drive car owners may enjoy the view without overextending themselves.

GETTING THERE: Drive east along Highway 7 past Harrison Mills, cross the Harrison River and go another 3.6 km to a side road on the left, across from Woodside Estates. A small tin shack is visible through the trees.

DESCRIPTION: Turn left (0 km), and take the good gravel road upwards through a series of switchbacks for 3.7 km, to a hang glider launching ramp. The trip is Class 1 to this point.

The road becomes a little more challenging, and at 7.8 km there is a campsite in the trees. The road levels out.

There is a fork at 10.0 km. The left branch climbs to a microwave tower and viewpoint about 1.6 km past Stacey Lake on the right. The right fork descends gradually, crossing several seasonal streamlets and a side road at 11.3 km.

The trail is now in a saddle between a bump and a rocky knob. At 13.1 km a side track doubles back to the left (don't bother). At 13.6 km, stop and enjoy a fine view of the valley to the east.

Between 14.2 and 14.6 km the trail is narrow and follows the mountainside.

There is another fork at 15.4 km. The left fork, on Class 3 rock, heads towards the lakes and a power line tower (which is mis-marked on most maps). The right fork is a bit rougher and culminates at the crest of a ridge (17.0 km). A track does continue down the side of the mountain, but ends at the last power transmission tower.

HARRISON–LILLOOET LAKE ROAD
Rating: 1

The Harrison–Lillooet Lake Road is not, strictly speaking, a four-wheel drive road at all (although its length and roughness make it a formidable trip). The two lakes, Harrison and Lillooet, are large enough to provides a beautiful foreground to the mountains on either side. A thick network of logging roads on either side of the main line, built over the last eighty or ninety years, provide a number of short, challenging four-wheel drive trips.

The twin-spired cathedral on the Skookumchuk Reserve is a favourite of photographers, and the massive operations of the active logging camps are interesting to observe. The road culminates in Mount Currie, and travellers may either continue over the Duffey Lake Road to Lillooet or return to Vancouver through Whistler and Squamish. There are quite a number of campsites along the road, either by the lakes or along the river.

GETTING THERE: Drive along Highway 7 to the Sasquatch Inn at Harrison Mills, and turn north along the paved road leading to Hemlock Valley.

The road system has changed in the past six or seven years. Now the standard route is to follow the west side of Harrison Lake past Tipella camp and then cross over to the east side and follow it up the Lillooet River and beside the lake to the junction with the Duffey Lake Road. However, there is also a road that goes a long way on the west side of Lillooet Lake, and a bridge across at Tena. Most of the logging is being done on the west side. Someday this side may offer a new network of roads. Distances in this section should, because of the length, be considered only approximate.

DESCRIPTION: Turn north at the Sasquatch Inn (0 km).
    0.4 km   Stay right along the main road.
    4.1 km   Cross Pretty Creek.

5.7 km	Bridge and campsite.
6.6 km	Chehalis Cafe. Stay left.
7.7 km	Stay right past Hemlock Valley Ski Area turn-off. There are several side paths off the Hemlock Road which are often used for off-road rallies.
11.3 km	Pavement ends.
12.6 km	Pass turn-offs to Weaver, Wolfe and Grace lakes.
18.3 km	Pass turn-off to Francis Lake.
23.3 km	Cross Carmell Creek.
30.1 km	Woods Lake campsite.
33.4 km	Interesting side road to left.
33.8 km	Hale Creek (popular 4 X 4 route). Several side paths of varied difficulty may be found up this branch.
35.4 km	Side road left to Sunrise Lake (links with Hale Creek).
39.0 km	Stay right past Mystery Creek Road, which connects with the Chehalis system.
42.7 km	Side road right down to 20 Mile Bay. Usually closed.
43.7 km	Bridge over 20 Mile Creek.
43.9 km	Road right to 20 Mile Bay. Usually closed.
45.0 km	Stay right.
54.7 km	Cross Davidson Creek. Level area.
63.8 km	Bremner Creek. From this point forward the road becomes much rougher. A couple of short sections will tempt drivers to use four-wheel drive. Cross bridges and eventually drop down into the Tipella logging camp.

81.1 km	Tipella logging operation. Extensive machinery and equipment, and an office where travellers should register. They will warn logging trucks to watch out for you. Note that the logging trucks in this area use extra-wide beds; one would not want to get caught on a tight corner.
85.1 km	Stay left.
87.8 km	Stay right. Left to Sloquet Hot Springs.
90.3 km	Junction. Stay right to cross bridge to west side.
94.7 km	Road enters at right from Metals Research.
96.3 km	Stay left.
109.1 km	Whiskey Lake.
110.8 km	Gowan Creek.
114.3 km	Skookumchuk village. Pass a car graveyard on left. Note the turn-of-the-century wooden cathedral.
120.9 km	Stay left.
121.3 km	Rogers Creek, followed shortly by a rough section.
136.8 km	Turn-off (left) to Tena Bridge. Stay right.
143.0 km	Houses to right.
147.0 km	Driftwood Bay campsite.
146.5 km	Cross Lizzie Creek. There are logging roads up both sides of the creek. Active logging.
148.2 km	Lizzie Creek campsite.
151.6 km	Twin Two Creek, followed by Twin One Creek.
156.3 km	Strawberry Point campsite.
162.5 km	Duffey Lake Road junction. Left to Mount Currie, right to Duffey Lake.

SLOQUET HOT SPRINGS
Rating: 6

A long and sometimes rugged drive just for a hot bath—
but oh, what a bath! Two pools, one hot and one hotter,
beside the rushing white water of a mountain stream

Waterfall, Harrison Lake area (Keith Thirkell photo)

surrounded by second-growth forest. The cares of the city seem far, far away. That is, if the place is not crowded. There is one major obstacle: a stream crossing, slightly over 2.0 km short of the springs. You may wish to leave your truck, wade the stream, and hike to the bathing area.

GETTING THERE: Drive Highway 7 to the Sasquatch Inn, and turn north up Harrison Lake. Wind your way up the lake past Tipella logging camp (register at the office if you value your life), a total of 88.0 km from the Sasquatch Inn. The Sloquet turn-off (left) is about 5.0 km north of the logging camp.

DESCRIPTION: Take the turn-off to the left (0 km) just past Sloquet Creek crossing. The trail is immediately rough—washed, worn and rocky—but soon improves and levels out.

At 2.3 km there is a nice view of the creek to the left.

An older logged area at 3.6 km has become a pleasant meadow that must also be popular with the local bears.

A washout requiring a little four-wheel drive effort is at 3.8 km.

Go back into the trees at 5.3 km, passing an old camp on the left.

At 5.4 km cross a major stream by a ford. The consensus of recent visitors to this spot is that the stream has become much deeper, and several four-wheelers were loath to try it. Wade it first. There is a one-truck campsite beside the stream. Beyond the creek, the trail passes through a forest glade.

Come to a clearing and campsite at 8.3 km. A steep, rutted road leads from the clearing to a lower campsite, several hundred yards closer to the hot springs. This second campsite is out of view, and I recommend walking down to see if there is any room there before driving down. It would be a shame to drive down this last section only to have to drive back up again.

From the second, or lower, campsite, a footpath leads to

Sloquet Creek and the sulphurous steam of the hot springs. The pools are reached by walking a log to the left, and following a path to a rocky beach right beside the water. The foliage—ferns—gives the place a tropical atmosphere. Some good soul has constructed two pools, and the area is quite neat and tidy. Keep it that way. Pack home your debris.

 COGBURN CREEK
Rating: 3–4

The old Cogburn Creek logging road was gated for many years, and the rumour got round that it stretched "within a few hundred yards of the Emory Creek road," and almost, but not quite, enabled direct access to the Fraser Canyon. Unable to resist any credible tale about a cross-watershed route, we started out early on a May morning to explore the area.

GETTING THERE: From Harrison Hot Springs (0 km) drive north along the lake through Sasquatch Park to the Harrison East Forest Service Road (6 km) and stay left. Cross bridges and pass waterfalls at approximately 7 and 15 km. Pass the Bear Creek Forest Road on the right at 17 km. At 23 km come to Pretty's Bear Creek logging operation and continue on the main road to the intersection at 24.5 km.

DESCRIPTION: Take the left intersection (0 km) and cross Cogburn Creek, turning right on the other side of the bridge. The trail follows the creek, and there are several small campsites and pullouts frequented by weekend recreationists.

The road has not been maintained; there is a small washout to cross at 2.2 km and a rather tattered bridge at 3.5 km. At 4 km stay right (an old sign reads "3 miles"). The valley narrows with a rock wall on the left.

At 6.2 come to a fork. The right fork leads up the slopes

above Settler Creek towards Old Settler Mountain, but is blocked by a washout and logs at 2.5 km. Take the left fork to continue up Cogburn Creek.

At 7.3 cross a bridge over a side stream, and come to a clearing. At 12 km a side road enters from the right, and at 13 km the road swings right over a pretty stream. The road enters into a high open valley at 17 km and the views improve, although the roadbed becomes quite a bit rougher. I stayed left at the fork and headed for the head of the valley at 24 km.

Although there was still snow in the trees at the head of the valley, it seemed clear to me that no road continues up the headwall and over to the Fraser Canyon. Hikers, however, might find a pretty good view from the ridge.

CLEAR CREEK HOTSPRINGS
Rating: 7–8

With each edition of this book the Clear Creek Hot Springs trail becomes more and more difficult. Trusted colleagues report that winching is now mandatory, and that the "rock crawling" of yore is now more like climbing a waterfall. The author of this deterioration is water. Hillside runoff has concentrated on the old road bed, rapidly wearing it away and making it nearly impassable. No one really talks about the pleasures of the hot springs any more; they are simply glad to get home with only a few serious scrapes and dents.

GETTING THERE: Drive to Harrison Hot Springs and take the road running along the lake to the east. Pass the Cascade Peninsula turn-off, Bear Creek at 17 km, and Pretty's logging operation at 23 km, all on a two-lane graded road. After circumventing the camp, pass the Cogburn turn off at 24.5 km, staying left. Cross through the G & F Logging camp, and continue onto an old airstrip, staying left at 36 km, and then right onto the Clear Creek road at 38 km (0 km).

DESCRIPTION: The right fork angles uphill, entering the Clear Creek valley and following the stream. It is sandy at first, then a lot rougher. At 4 km and 7 km the stream has done its work.

The hardest section is beyond the bridge to the right (stay left) at 8 km. From here on out it is pure muscle to the bridge at 10 km, which is about one kilometre from the cabin and hot tubs.

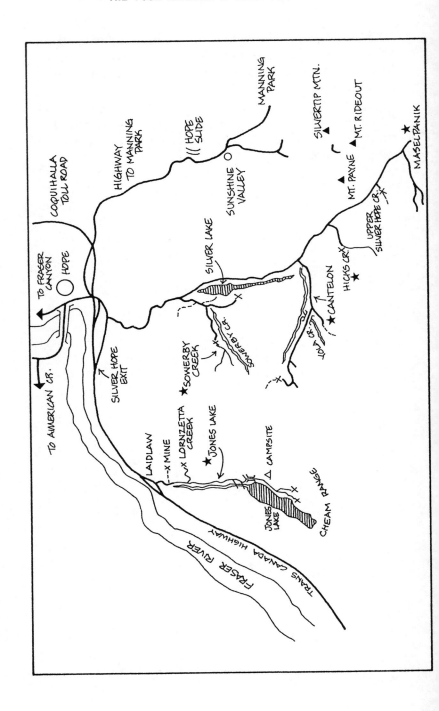

Section 4
HOPE AREA

Hope seems as natural a starting point now as it did 130 years ago when it was the place to embark on journeys to the Interior. Two main highways (Trans-Canada and Highway 7) meet at Hope, and three highways fan out from Hope (Fraser Canyon/Highway 1, Coquihalla/Highway 3, and Hope-Princeton/Highway 5). Visitors will find a full range of services and, if they search a little, some four-wheeling.

The main area of interest is the Skagit Valley. Not so long ago, thousands of public-spirited citizens managed to protect the valley from flooding by a Washington State power company. Today it is the domain of logging companies and recreationists. Both have tended to over-use the area.

JONES LAKE
Rating: 1–2

The parking lot at Jones Lake (Waleach Lake on some maps) is often full of 4 X 4 vehicles. Not, I think, for the four-wheeling so much as the fishing. On the other hand, this BC Hydro access road is a fun little climb. There is also a private lodge at the lake for more settled vacationers. The road has been improved and presents no great difficulty.

GETTING THERE: Drive the Trans-Canada (Highway 1) to the Laidlaw turn-off, and bear right. Follow the paved road past a junction, heading back west to the sign that reads "Jones Lake Lodge 6½ Miles" (0 km), and follow the road beyond.

DESCRIPTION: From 0 km the road ascends steeply, causing some of those in cars to stop immediately and tarry at the stream on the right rather than go any farther.

A side road to the left (1.0 km) through the elderberry bushes is kept barely passable by someone with a mining claim. Two old shafts into the side of the mountain a few hundred yards into the bush testify to the belief that precious minerals—or the dream of them—exist in the area. (It was not uncommon, not so long ago, for unscrupulous businessmen to salt streams in this area).

A left turn on a side road at 1.5 km leads to Lornzetta Creek. This well-maintained road climbs and winds around the mountainside to the east, and apparently ascends Lornzetta Creek (reportedly beautiful). Unfortunately, it is securely locked and gated just when the road gets interesting. Try phoning 823-6621 for information on how to get the gate opened.

As the Jones Lake Road continues to climb along the mountainside to the left of Jones Creek, there are side roads to the right at 4.3 km and 6.8 km. The second may be an alternative route to the lake and the mountains across the lake.

There's a side road to the left at 7.7 km.

Cross a bridge at 8.2 km.

Jones Lake is at 8.3 km.

Beyond the parking lot the trail continues, mostly through thick bush, past the lodge. The fork to the left comes to a dead end 5.0 km farther on, at the beginning of a trail. A side road to the right leads to a washed-out bridge at one of the coves near the end of the lake.

SOWERBY CREEK
Rating: 3–4

With most of the side valleys inaccessible, Sowerby Creek looks inviting. If it goes through to the end of the valley, it might provide a way of getting to the high ridges or some small lakes. I haven't been that far.

GETTING THERE: Drive Highway 1 towards Hope, leave the new highway at the Silverhope exit, and then turn right along the Ross Lake (Skagit Valley) Road. A little over 5.0 km along the road take the Silver Lake branch (right), and at 6.8 km find the trailhead on the right (0 km).

DESCRIPTION: The trail follows the west side of the creek and is a bit bumpy. Almost immediately it comes to a fork, with the newer road going to the right. (The left is a bit steep and slanting—and probably worth exploring.)

Stay right at 1.4 km and cross a Bailey bridge over a stream.

At 2.7 km, cross an old bridge with bushes sprouting from the side rails, and continue up the rocky slope to a rock slide at 2.8 km. I was halted here by a couple of hog-sized boulders, big enough to stop a solo four-wheeler, but not so large that a small crew could not push them aside.

CANTELON CREEK
Rating: 3

The upper reaches of Cantelon Creek are being logged, and the road may not always be open, but the valley is worth exploring. The name comes from the family who logged the area, one of whom was killed in an accident. Watch for the memorial marker.

The valley splits into two branches, with the northern branch dividing again beneath the shoulders of Mount Ling. The southern branch curves beneath the slopes of Mount Northgraves and continues to a headwall below Goetz Peak and Williams Peak.

The swampy ground in this area breeds mosquitos, some of them so big that they don't suck but bite off chunks of flesh and fly back to the bushes with them. At least, that's what the old-timers say.

GETTING THERE: Take Highway 1 to the Silverhope exit, then go up the Silverhope (Skagit Valley) Road to an old logging sign, "20 km," and a right turn (0 km).

DESCRIPTION: From 0 km there is a rough but graded road through an area that is currently being logged. Stay left at the first fork.

Using a tug strap at Cantelon Creek

At 2.7 km stay right. (The left fork presumably leads up Yola Creek.)

Cross a creek on a new bridge at 3.6 km, and the stream is now on your left.

By 4.4 km the road is ascending the valley beside a beautiful whitewater stream that flows over a series of smooth, multi-coloured granite slabs. There are a number of nearly perfect spots for picnics and foot dabbling.

At 5.8 km you will pass a wrecked blue van which looks like it may have been an old mobile kitchen.

Stay right on the main road at 6.4 km.

Cross a bridge at 7.5 km, and pass more abandoned logging equipment.

The left branch at 8.0 km leads to active logging in less than a kilometre, and appears to head towards the alpine forest on the flanks of Mount Northgraves to the left.

The right branch strikes north up the slope, and in .6 km is blocked by a large rotten log. This way is probably passable, and leads higher up into the valley beneath the summit of Mount Ling.

 HICKS CREEK
Rating: 2–5

A washed-out bridge over a rushing stream makes a considerable difference in the rating of this trip. Getting across this section requires skill, tenacity and luck. But the road before and after this rough spot is relatively tame.

GETTING THERE: Drive up the Skagit, past the Cantelon Creek turn-off, and continue for approximately 4 km past a campground on the left, to the turn-off on the right (0 km).

DESCRIPTION: Follow the road along the flats, through a gate and start up the west side of the valley. The road gradually climbs to a fork at a bridge across a side stream (4 km). It took some rock moving and digging to get across, and even then it was pretty tricky.

Once across this barrier the trail deteriorates, but remains passable. We were halted at a log dump at 8 km. According to the maps, a trail should begin here which leads to Greendrop Lake and then drops down to the Chilliwack River Valley.

A rough section of the trail at Hicks Creek

Checking out a washout, Hicks Creek

 MASELPANIK CREEK
Rating: 2

Maselpanik Creek drains the basins beneath Mount Rahm and Mount Custer on the Canada/US border near the old Whatcom Trail Pass. Once gated, this road is now open.

GETTING THERE: From Highway 1, take the Silverhope exit (Exit 168) and turn right up Silverhope Creek just before the bridge. Follow the Skagit Valley for 33 km and look for a road into the trees on the right.

DESCRIPTION: From the turn-off (0 km), this main line logging road curves south and ascends into a wide valley. Around the 8.0 km mark, there is a branch to the left, which

71

Maselpanik Creek Road

crosses to the other side of the valley but then dead-ends. A bit farther, another track goes left, crosses Maselpanik Creek and parallels the main road.

The main road continues up the valley. It is mostly smooth with a few shallow drainage ditches. At 12.0 km, a worn trail veers right. This looks like a good spot to start a hike into the high country and perhaps the summit of Mount Thompson.

At 14.0 km a trail heads off to the right towards the Whatcom Pass.

The main road drops down into a basin with views of Camp Peak and Mount Rahm. The road ends at 16.0 km. There is much evidence of logging but by 1989 there was no active logging. This is probably a popular destination for hunters.

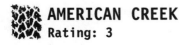 AMERICAN CREEK
Rating: 3

The American Creek valley has been used by just about everybody. The mountainsides have been logged; shake cutters have attacked the remains. A bewildering array of high tension powerlines swing from tower to tower, dancing from one side of the valley to the other. All of these activities have left off-road possibilities.

This route changes enormously according to the season. During late summer, most of the stream beds are dry and present no more problems than a little bouncing; during the wet season, these crossings can be a lot harder. I have had one near-accident in which a wet shoulder on a spur road nearly collapsed beneath me.

GETTING THERE: From Hope take Highway 1, crossing the Fraser River at the western edge of town, and joining Highway 7. The turn-off to American Creek (signed) is about 4 km from this intersection, just past Schkam Lake. Turn left, come to a clearing, and take the middle path uphill (0 km).

DESCRIPTION: Turn off the highway (0 km), pass the sheds at the intersection and skirt the hillside, gradually ascending on a dirt road with a few lumpy places. Pass a side road coming in from the right at 1.4 km.

Drive under the power lines at 3.0 km, and a branch road drops to the right. Bypass it—this goes down the other side of American Creek and connects American Creek with Emory Creek.

Cross a good bridge at 4.6 km. Just before this, a side road takes off into the bushes to the left but ends a little way up the mountain. Others have tried it, probably looking for the old road allegedly leading to Dog Mountain.

The road is now curving up the valley amidst the power lines and the peculiar shaggy look of second-growth timber. The punk-cut mountaintops and the white spines of some old trees give the country a weird appearance. There are too many small watercourses to count, and a few dips in the road.

At 7.5 km there is a major fork. The left goes up a

network of logging roads on the ridge to the south. The right heads downhill (and is marked by a pile of rocks) and is the correct route. Once again it is necessary to cross several seasonal streamlets.

The trail now swings around to the right and crosses a nearly obscure bridge (9.5 km) before swinging left again. A couple of branches to explore enter from the right.

At 10.8 km there is another fork. The left fork crosses a bush-covered bridge and zigzags up the slope to the south, providing a good view of the pond. The right fork is apparently less travelled, but is the correct one. A new offshoot to the right at 11.9 km only goes a few hundred yards.

At 12.4 km the road drops down and skirts the west end of the pond. A short side road to the right leads to a camping spot. This brackish pond has a number of photographic possibilities.

Note: If you decide to continue past the pond, be careful. The trail descends quickly and becomes very rough. The section past the pylon at 14.6 once led out to Harrison Lake. Now it is impassable.

SQUEAH ROAD
Rating: 1–2

Squeah is an old townsite and logging camp on the east bank of the Fraser River. In the 1930s it was home to a number of unemployed men who fled from the city and lived along the CN tracks. Later it was a logging camp with a shop, boat dock, sheds and bunkhouses. For many years it was simply abandoned, but now there are a couple of residents living in one of the cabins.

The road presents few difficulties, but provides an interesting glimpse of the Fraser from the eastern bank, and a museum of old equipment.

GETTING THERE: Drive into Hope and turn onto 6th Avenue at the softball park (0 km).

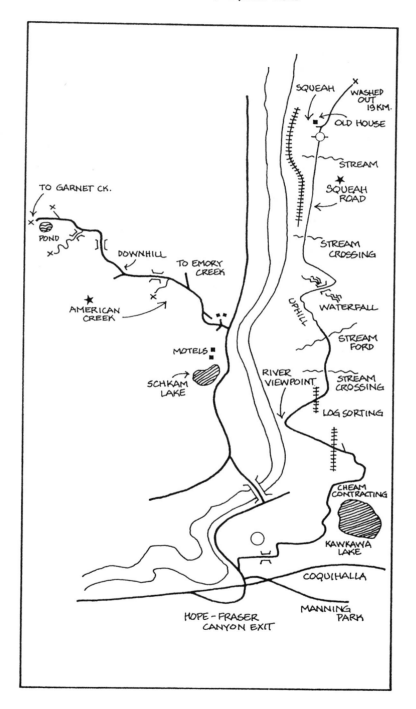

An abandoned logging camp building on the Squeah Road

DESCRIPTION: Drive east, crossing the Coquihalla River, and turn left onto Union Bar Road towards Kawkawa Lake.

Drive along the mountainside to the north of Kawkawa Lake on a good gravel road. A logging company office is located at 4 km. Check in, if necessary, and turn left.

Pass through a log sorting area at 5 km, stay left at 6.5 km, cross the CN tracks at 6.6 km, and go right.

At 7.1 km cross the log sorting area, diagonally to the right, and angle towards the telephone poles beside the railway tracks. Cross the tracks and continue up the road.

Cross the stream at 10.5 km, and follow the mountainside on your right. Ignore a side road at 12.1 km and stay right and uphill. Cross another stream and climb to the top of the hill.

The trail drops back down again at 15.2 km, crosses a stream and then traverses a rock face. There is a nice waterfall just above the bridge, hidden in the rocks.

Cross Squeah Creek at 15.7, and through a gate and rusting metal at 17.4. If the gate is closed, you can probably walk the rest of the way to the old logging camp.

The road beyond the camp continues uphill. It is washed out, and eventually blocked by an enormous slide. An eroded clearcut hill simply slumped, taking out the road.

Note: Vandals have had a field day with the old equipment. Whatever urge causes grown men and women to destroy just because no one is looking, should be stifled. Vandalism in the form of thievery. Blasting away with shotguns, breaking windows, tearing apart cabins is a major reason why four-wheelers often find roads gated.

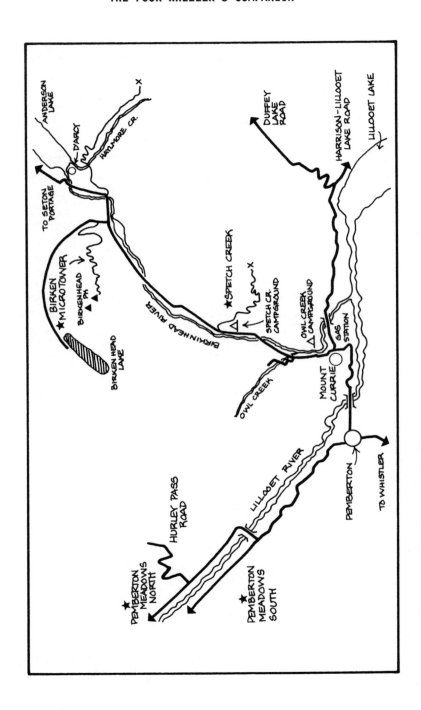

Section 5
PEMBERTON AREA

On almost any summer weekend, the main intersection in Pemberton is a hive of activity. The Whistler crowd is checking out the other side of the tracks, loggers and potato farmers are doing their weekly shopping, and four-wheelers are fueling up for a day on the back roads. From Pemberton, roads connected to smaller trails fan out in all directions.

The Pemberton Valley, famous for its potatoes and floods, stretches towards the latest logging operation and the virtually untouched glaciers and peaks of the Coast Range. The main road up the valley leads party animals to Meager Creek Hot Springs, and others to Hurley Pass. Hurley Pass, once a tough graded road, has now been tamed sufficiently that most cars will have no difficulty reaching Gold Bridge during the dry season, but the steep hairpin curves on the first section still make one glad that a 4 X 4 has low gearing.

From the intersection at the east edge of Pemberton, a good paved road leads northeast through Mount Currie and towards D'Arcy. Possibilities for exploration off the

D'Arcy road include Owl Lake, Birkenhead Provincial Park, and the steep valleys above Anderson Lake. From D'Arcy a twisting power line road follows Anderson Lake to Seton Portage, where it is possible to buy a t-shirt at a pub boasting that you have driven the "Hi-Line" road. From Seton Portage the road climbs to Mission Pass and over to Carpenter Lake and eventually Gold Bridge (west) or Lillooet (east).

The most popular road is the Duffey Lake Road, which stretches from the Mount Currie Reserve to Lillooet. The section through the Reserve is unpaved, but the rest of the road is paved. Logging roads extend outward from the Duffey Lake Road up nearly every subsidiary valley. Opportunities for hikers abound in this area; many of the branch logging roads and old mining roads reach timberline. Just east of the Reserve, the Harrison–Lillooet Road branches to the right and follows the lakes past several subsidiary valleys.

If you plan to try some of the trails below, be sure to fill your gas tanks in Pemberton or Mount Currie (noting that both stations are often closed in the evening), since the next set of pumps is a long way off.

PEMBERTON MEADOWS–SOUTH SIDE
Rating: 1–2

One look at the Lillooet River west of Pemberton tells you that this great meandering river is subject to flooding. Over the years, roads and bridges have been rebuilt many times. The current standard route now follows the south side of the river for the first 24.0 km, before crossing over to the north side. On the north side one may drive up the Pemberton Valley until stopped by logging, or may turn north and climb over Hurley Pass to Gold Bridge. Those who take the old road, which continues along the south side, have usually made a wrong turn somewhere.

On the other hand, the south bank road is an easy trip with many picnic spots, good views of the mountains, and an abundance of wildlife. On a cloudy afternoon we came

Pemberton Meadows, south side (Keith Thirkell photo)

across several deer, a very heavy-duty black bear standing on a pile of logs, a coyote creeping across the road and a wide variety of birds.

The road follows the river to a washout and presents no great difficulty, although early in the year there are undoubtedly many wet spots.

GETTING THERE: Drive to Pemberton and the intersection at the Scotia Bank (Birch at Prospect), and turn right (west).

DESCRIPTION: From the intersection (0 km) drive west along the south bank of the river, passing the turn-off (right) to Meager Creek and Hurley Pass at 23.0 km, and stay straight ahead.

At 22.7 km the paved road turns to gravel.

Cross a bridge over a creek at 23.4 km.

At 38.5 km cross a new bridge over a frequently flooded

creek bed (the presence of a new bridge suggests that some improvement of this road is contemplated).

Stay left at the fork at 38.6 km.

Stay right at the fork at 42.0 km.

The end of the road is at 46.7 km. The river has carved out the bank and a stream bed, and has carried the bridge away. Until someone replaces the bridge or digs a ford, this is as far as one can go.

PEMBERTON MEADOWS NORTH
Rating: 1–2

Most travellers taking the road along the north side of the meadows are in a hurry to climb Hurley Pass and head for Gold Bridge. Instead of taking the Hurley Pass turn-off, the four-wheeler may like to continue up the Pemberton Valley to the end of the road. A washed-out Bailey bridge prevents a very deep penetration of the valley, but the countryside is nice and is not frequently travelled.

GETTING THERE: Drive to Pemberton and into town, turn right at the Scotia Bank, and continue on the paved road to the Hurley turn-off (marked) at about 23.0 km.

DESCRIPTION: From the Hurley turn-off (0 km) travel 7.2 km on the dirt road, crossing the Lillooet River, to the road branching right up Hurley Pass. Stay left.

There is a bridge and a side road to the right at 8.4 km. There is another bridge at 9.9 km.

At 15.9 km and 17.7 km there are roads to the right.

At 27.2 km there is a road to the right marked "CBR10." These roads appear to be spurs for the logging operations on the mountainsides. We haven't explored them, but it does not look as if any of them go over the mountains—only to the dead ends below the ridges. There is a bridge at 32.9 km.

The road to the left at 35.6 km goes to Meager Creek Hot

Springs, popular for parties, and unpopular with the loggers for that reason.

Continuing to the right, stay left at 36.1 and 36.2 km.

At 37.0 km there is a bridge and a track to the river.

Cross a creek at 41.1 km and start uphill.

Cross another creek at 45.5 km and come to a bridge with a waterfall upstream at 46.2 km.

The road is washed out (bridge out) at 46.8 km, although it is possible to hoof it for another 2.0 km to the broken Bailey bridge across the river.

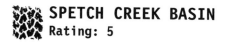 SPETCH CREEK BASIN
Rating: 5

This short run provides room for some low-range rock crawling and some pretty good views of the valley between Mount Currie and D'Arcy. The weekend we visited the area, we passed several cars parked on the lower section of the road. Clearly the owners were hiking up the basin and over a col (a small mountain pass or saddle) to some lakes on the other side, beneath the glaciers. After following the road to its end, we felt sorry for the hikers; they had walked up a driveable trail for several bushy kilometres, only to face a difficult bushwhack through uncut forest at the end. Perhaps the lakes and high country above made the effort worth it.

GETTING THERE: Drive to the intersection just outside Pemberton, and take the highway right to Mount Currie. Do not turn off to Duffey Lake from Mount Currie, but continue straight (30 kph) through the village and north up the valley towards D'Arcy. From the centre of Mount Currie (intersection with Duffey Lake Road) it is approximately 12.2 km along a paved road to the Spetch Creek campsite on the right (poorly marked with a small sign). Pass the campsite and the rather florid gates of a private residence, and take the next turn north on the right. This gravel road doubles back behind Spetch Creek campsite and up to the basin.

DESCRIPTION: Turn right onto the gravel road (0 km). At first the road is not steep, but it gradually becomes more so as you pass behind the Spetch Creek campsite. Continue straight at 1.8 km.

Most drivers of two-wheel drive cars, having climbed the hill, decide to call it quits at the clearing at 2.0 km. Four minor obstacles present themselves: a rocky stream crossing, a small section of corduroy road, some rocks and a rather shaky little bridge. They are easily surmounted.

At 2.1 km ignore the branch to the left.

The roadway is filling with a screen of new growth at 3.8 km, and it is hard to see very far ahead. The cool air and the sound of rushing water suggest a stream crossing and, indeed, there is a bridge. It is worth stopping to make sure before rumbling across it. After this crossing of Spetch Creek, the road becomes progressively rougher and more overgrown.

The first switchback is at 4.2 km. The road heads into a small basin, then curves back and up the slope to the next basin. This happens several times. Each time the road is a little worse. By the time you have gone 5.6 km, most of the switchback curves are pretty worn and there are some camouflaged dips along the straight stretches. In a couple of spots, winter rains have gullied both sides of the road.

5.9 km may be the place to stop, especially if you plan to hike farther and try to reach the lakes above. The next switchbacks enter some very thick bushes, and the road ends at 7.9 km in a clearing on the mountainside.

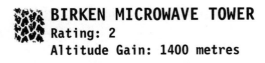

BIRKEN MICROWAVE TOWER
Rating: 2
Altitude Gain: 1400 metres

It was one of those gorgeously warm and clear August weekends when we spent the night on this mountaintop. All the wildflowers seemed to be in bloom, and as dusk fell, the cool air wafted the faint scents around the campsite. We lounged in our folding chairs, watching the gradually setting sun shift the shadows on the rugged peaks and glaciers across the valley. Several squadrons of mosquitos failed to diminish the tranquility of the spot.

In the morning we hiked around the rocks of the mountainside, peeking at the great walled basin to the north, and eventually ended up on a small meadow looking south towards Mount Currie. The summer heat discouraged further hiking, so we retreated back to the trucks and down the steep winding road to the valley floor.

The surface of the microwave tower road is quite good, but it is very steep and a long haul. If your vehicle tends to heat up, you might want to pass this one by. No one needs to be reminded that micro transmission equipment is expensive and the penalties for messing around with it are quite severe. Use the road for the trip, enjoy the view, and leave the buildings alone.

GETTING THERE: Drive north from Mount Currie towards D'Arcy, and take the turn-off to Birkenhead Lake.

DESCRIPTION: From the turn-off (0 km), follow the Birkenhead Lake Road for .8 km and then go left up a road marked "Logging." There is a bit of logging up above, but this road is mainly used to service the microwave tower.

The road starts to switchback steeply almost immediately. Pass logging operations at 4.8 km, stay left at 5.3 km and right at 5.7 km. The road now switches to the east slope and continues upward to the parking area at the tower, at 10.1 km.

A trail continues to a clearing a little farther up the shoulder of the mountain. Since it provides additional views, it is worth the walk.

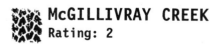 **McGILLIVRAY CREEK**
Rating: 2

There is nothing to stop a four-wheeler from following McGillivray Creek to its headwaters, then connecting with

Cadwallader Creek and driving into Bralorne. Nothing except trees. But McGillivray Creek is being actively logged and the road extended. Someday, perhaps, there will be an alternative to Hurley Pass. Presently, however it is a short road into a high valley.

GETTING THERE: Drive from Mount Currie to just south of D'Arcy and take the Hi Line road to Seton Portage/Shalath (signed). Follow the Hi-Line road for 9 km (stay left at 6.7 km) and take the logging road to the left (0 km).

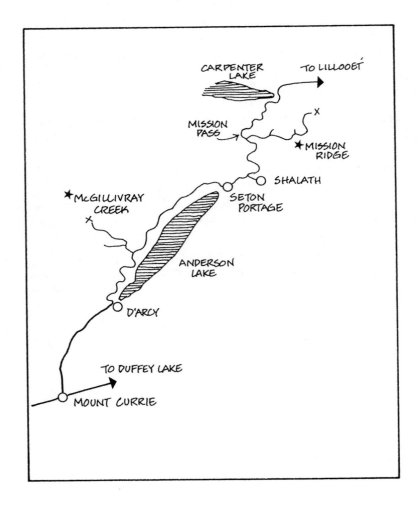

DESCRIPTION: The road starts uphill and almost immediately branches. Cross the bridge and stay left.

The road climbs along the mountainside above the valley floor for 5 km and ends wherever the D-9 and grader have left off for the day. I could see a road along the valley floor, but it did not seem to go as far up the valley. According to the maps, there is a hiking trail from the end of the road, over the pass, to Cadwallader Creek.

MISSION RIDGE
Rating: 2–3

It takes considerable stamina to negotiate the Hi-Line road from D'Arcy to Seton Portage. This powerline road is dusty, narrow, with some awesome drop-offs. Drive carefully, particularly on the many blind corners. This is a popular route for dirt bikers. Seton Portage is a sleepy little railway village with a couple of places to eat, and not much else. The road up to Mission Pass beside the great conduits bringing water from Carpenter Lake is all uphill, but in good condition.

GETTING THERE: Go from Mount Currie to D'Arcy, from D'Arcy to Seton Portage on the Hi-Line Road, through Seton Portage and up the mountainside to the pass. The Mission Ridge trail starts just south of the pass to the right (0 km).

DESCRIPTION: The trail climbs steeply to the ridge. Along the ridge you will pass one small and two larger microwave towers. Pass the first tower and stay on the main road past the turnoff to the second by keeping left.

As you approach the third microwave tower (6.5 km), a side road right leads downhill. The road becomes a little rougher, drops down to a small col, and then swings to the left along the mountainside beside a set of powerlines. Distant ridgelines tinted in various shades of blue and green are visible in every direction.

A snowdrift on the road at Mission Pass

As the road reaches the end of the ridge, it swings right. I was stopped by snowbanks here (in mid-June) at 9 km. Apparently the trail curves to the right around the ridge, then traverses the basin on the other side. However, a major landslide has wiped it out, and it is impassable.

If you decide to continue over Mission Pass and down to Carpenter Lake (steep, but well maintained), there is a campsite at the end of the Tergazi dam near the outflow.

 BLOWDOWN PASS
Rating: 3

The Blowdown Pass Road demonstrates why old mining roads are often preferable to old logging roads. Many logging roads start out in the direction of some interesting or intriguing place, only to end before you get there. Logging regulations (and arbitrary jurisdictional lines) usually prohibit the extension of a logging road to the tree line. Mining roads, on the other hand, go directly to the source of the ore (or the dream of ore)—over passes if necessary.

The Blowdown Road goes over a high pass at 2100 metres above sea level. From here it is possible to hike back down to a pleasant little lake, up either ridge to small summits, or down the other side of the pass to the old Silver Queen Mine. Whether you are a hiker or not, the chance to drive out of the trees and into the high country is always exhilarating.

GETTING THERE: Drive from the turn-off to Mount Currie, through the L'il Wat Nation, and up the Duffey Lake Road past the lake to the campground. Continue past the campground around a couple of curves for about 2 km and look for a side road sharply to the right and uphill. It always takes me a couple of tries to find the turn-off.

DESCRIPTION: The first portion of the road is two-wheel drive—a main line logging road—and may be followed for 9 km, bypassing several spur roads on either side.

Looking west from Blowdown Pass

At 9.0 km stay left of the fork, switch into four-wheel drive and climb the side of the mountain using the short switchbacks. As you ascend, a small triangular alpine lake becomes visible on the valley floor—it is a popular, if buggy, campsite.

At 14.0 km the road is above the treeline and begins its final traverse towards the pass at 15.0 km. It is a short hike from this windy col to the summits on either side. Usually snow blocks the pass until late in the year.

If the road is clear, it is possible to head down into the basin. At 28.0 km the road crosses a stream and the trailhead to the Stein Valley (11 km on foot). The road beyond the stream heads uphill to the old mine.

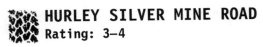 HURLEY SILVER MINE ROAD
Rating: 3–4

Travellers feed on rumours, amplify them, and turn them into exaggerated claims. Look, for example, at the earliest maps of North America, which showed all kinds of wishful thinking about rivers crossing the continent. Similarly, there has always been a rumour about "the road that runs from Duffey Lake to D'Arcy." If there is one, it is not the Hurley Mine Road—which is no reason not to take it. (It may also be worth noting that there is no connection, except in name, between the "Hurley Mine Road" and "Hurley Pass" to the west.)

This steep, narrow shelf road is subject to a lot of rockfall, and lots of extra effort is sometimes required to get around boulders that are too big to drive over, even with the largest tires. It ends in a high basin with several tracks fanning out up the slopes, leading to mining test holes. Another thing: there are bears in this valley.

GETTING THERE: Drive 51.1 km from Pemberton Junction, past Duffey Lake, to a bridge taking off to the left and a sign, "Hurley Silver Mine," at 0 km.

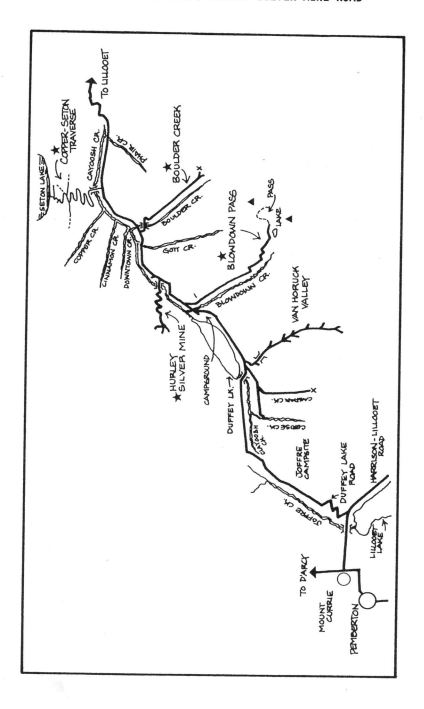

DESCRIPTION: From the end of the bridge, a good road starts uphill sharply, passing a secluded campsite, and switchbacks up the mountainside about ten times. (It is hard to keep count when you are dodging rocks in the path.)

Stay right at a spur at .2 km (it leads to a dead end).

Stay left at the fork at 2.8 km, and head back into the remaining trees. At 3.5 km cross the stream on a solid bridge and make one switchback, then head up into the upper valley. From here on out, the country is more and more open.

Just before entering the basin (approx. 7.0 km) there is a campsite beside a stream. The road continues up through sparse, low, sub-alpine trees into the basin. The branches in all directions lead nowhere, but provide the hiker with a means to reach the ridges.

It is true that from the north col you can see Haylmore Valley, but there isn't a driveable path—or at least we didn't

Along the Hurley Mine Road

find it. Who knows, maybe it was covered by snow. (Warning: the basin is full of terrific avalanche chutes, and even in early summer these can be dangerous.)

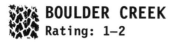 BOULDER CREEK
Rating: 1–2

One look at some roads and you know they won't last; they are here today but will be blown away tomorrow. Such is the case with the Boulder Creek Road. The first bridge over the tumbling creek will probably be wiped out during a spring runoff. And if this doesn't happen, rock slides on the far side will soon obliterate the switchbacks. Once active logging ceases, this backroad is a goner.

Some 13.5 km beyond the Hurley Silver Mine Road, as you drive east on the Duffey Lake Road, a large gash on the mountainside to the southeast is visible. The road is not as difficult as it looks, although rockfall makes it tricky, and it leads up a straight valley to a headwall of summits. From the upper reaches of the road it is possible to hike a few hundred feet up to timberline, and visit some marvellously unspoiled country.

GETTING THERE: From Pemberton drive over the Duffey Lake Road, past Duffey Lake and down along Cayoosh Creek. 18.0 km past the Duffey Lake campsite and past the Gott Creek sign, turn right onto a side road (marked) and start uphill (0 km).

DESCRIPTION: The road curves left and then right towards the stream, which it crosses at 1.4 km, over a good but tenuous bridge.

The road turns left (north) and begins to climb, switchbacking sharply over rough rock, then levels off and crosses a second bridge back to the west side of the valley at 2.9 km.

There are four more bridges crossing back and forth across the stream over the next couple of kilometres, and then the road settles down and follows the east side of the valley, gradually departing from the valley floor. The meandering creek may be seen below.

In several spots the country is open enough to provide a glimpse of the ridge line to the east, and the brush is not so thick as to deter a hiker from clambering up to the ridge. One of the shortest routes is just north of a small stream crossing at 13.0 km.

The road ends at 14.5 km in soon-to-be-cut forest. From the top of the ridge it looks as if it would be a short hike to reach timberline from this point. Getting down to the stream, however, looks a bit difficult.

We noticed evidence of some very large bears, perhaps grizzlies, and made sure to take the appropriate precautions when we camped.

COPPER CREEK TO SETON LAKE
Rating: 5

In the maze of ridges and valleys of the Cayoosh Range, south of Anderson and Seton lakes and north of the Duffey Lake Road, there seems to be only one through route. This logging track departs from the Duffey Lake Road by crossing a bridge near Copper Creek, and becomes a hair-raising shelf road that gains the top of the ridge. Beyond that, a series of very old and very steep logging roads (shown on old maps but not new ones) drops down to the power lines running along the south shore of Seton Lake. This is one of those trails where drivers will want to assure themselves that, having gone down, they can come back up. It would not be cheap or easy to bring a barge in from Lillooet to extract your vehicle.

GETTING THERE: Drive over the Duffey Lake Road, past the lake, and down Cayoosh Creek. Pass the Hurley Mine Road, Gott Creek, and the Cottonwood and Cinnamon campsites. The start of the trail is a bridge crossing Cayoosh Creek to the north (left), 1.1 km east of the Cinnamon campsite (0 km).

DESCRIPTION: After crossing the bridge, the road builds up steam by following Cayoosh Creek for a time, and then starts a stiff series of switchbacks and curves up the mountainside.

After three sharp switchbacks, the track curves precipitously around the side of the mountain to the east, then switchbacks again, and finally approaches the ridge at 6.1 km.

At the top of the ridge, in a log clearing area, there are several branches. The right track goes west along the ridge towards a summit. The left goes east along the ridge around a bump. The middle track heads north down the mountainside towards Seton Lake. Try the middle.

At 8.2 km there is another junction. The right is a dead end. The left drops into the trees. Follow the left track as it twists sharply and steeply down towards the lake. The main path gradually levels off and starts heading northwest (to a dead end), but a steep cut-off drops more directly down to the lake.

At 12.6 km you will come to the power line cut. By going straight ahead it is possible to drive to a very tiny (two-truck) campsite on the lake shore. Going right along the power line right-of-way takes you to a knoll (2.5 km) overlooking the lake. A spur to the right, back up the hill, will return you to the road above.

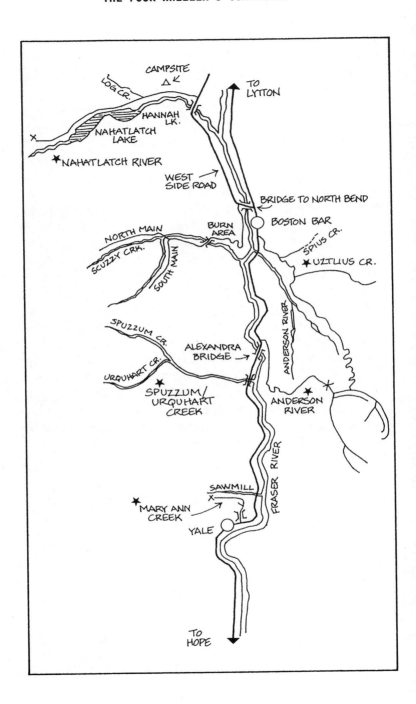

Section 6
FRASER CANYON

The Fraser Canyon is a narrow labyrinth of gorges funneling millions of gallons of fast running water from the Interior. In the 19th century rivers were viewed as natural pathways, but the Fraser mocked that sensible theory. In 1858 during the gold rush, every effort was made to find alternate ways to the gold fields, but despite its dangers, the canyon remained a key route. Today the tracks of the Canadian National and Canadian Pacific railways snake along both sides of the canyon, and above them, Highway 1 follows the canyon to Lytton and Lillooet. Traffic on the highway seems lighter since the opening of the Coquihalla Highway, and it is often a pleasure to drive.

Much of the four-wheeling in the area takes place from the West Side Road, which is reached by crossing the bridge at Boston Bar or taking the reaction ferry at Lytton. This little road from Boston Bar to Lillooet refuses to be civilized; it is nearly as rough and narrow now as it was in 1976, when I drove it in a VW bug. Some sections of the road drop off precipitously to the river, others wind in and out of dry forest land and run beside calm pastures. The four-wheel trails follow tributaries of the Fraser high into the mountains. The Scuzzy, Nahatlatch, and Kwoiek Creek roads do not cross the range, but the Kookipi logging road angles back to Harrison Lake.

On the east side, a number of logging roads penetrate the less dramatic but nonetheless challenging mountains between the Fraser and the Coquihalla. The Little Switzerland area, accessible via the Catermole Timber Co. road near Alexandra Bridge, is especially scenic. Farther north, the Utzlius Creek Forest Road ascends the watershed and then follows Spius Creek down to the Coquihalla. The Botanie Valley, north of Lytton, has long been a favourite of backroaders, especially in early summer when the wildflowers carpet the upper meadows.

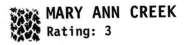

MARY ANN CREEK
Rating: 3

This trail once led to Inkawthia Lake, but no more. The old ford has long since become a pile of boulders and the track on the other side is totally overgrown. This makes for a short trip.

GETTING THERE: Drive from Hope to Yale. Look for Albert Road (a street sign). A right turn onto Albert Road will take you to the local museum and the plaque commemorating the Chinese workers who were paid a dollar a day to build the railway. A turn to the left (0 km) passes the local library and crosses a small stream starting uphill.

DESCRIPTION: The road zigzags up, passing under the powerline a couple of times, before coming to a fork at 3.5 km. The left (uphill) is probably the Sawmill Creek Road; the right (downhill) is the one we followed.

At 4.4 km there is a track leading off to the right, but it is only a service road for the powerline, so stay straight. The road becomes a little rougher and more overgrown.

At 5.3 stay left, and at 8.4 come to a turnaround. You can see the stream and the old ford, but not much else.

I tried several side paths in the area, mostly on the right, but none went anywhere.

SPUZZUM–URQUHART CREEK
Class: 3–4

I was led to explore this watershed by rumours that a new logging road now linked Urquhart Creek with Hornet Creek on the Harrison Lake side of the mountain. The col between the two watersheds does not look very steep on the topographical map, so the rumour had some plausibility. As it turned out, neither fork of the Urquhart reaches the headwall, but the upper valleys are broad and Mount Urquhart has a photogenic granite ridge.

GETTING THERE: Drive north from Yale for 14 km past the Reserve, cross Spuzzum Creek, and turn left onto the Spuzzum Forest Road (0 km).

DESCRIPTION: A reasonably good road climbs steeply for the first 5 km, crossing a bridge at 4.6 km. Since this is an active forest road, I worried about meeting a logging truck coming downhill.

At 6 km the road begins to level out, following the valley. At 10.5 there is a major fork. The right fork is an active main line logging road. If the rumour of a watershed crossing is true, then it may be along this road. However, I stayed left, crossed a bridge and continued to climb. This section of the road is not being actively logged, and many ditches have been dug across it.

At 13.1 km I came to another fork. This time I stayed right and followed the main valley. I forded a stream at 15.5 km and came to a dead end at 16 km. This seemed odd to me since I could see log patches off in the distance, but no obvious road to them. The spot does provide a good glimpse of Mount Urquhart.

I retreated to 13.1 km and followed the left fork for another 3.5 km before being stopped by a washout. Nevertheless, I could see that the road did not continue up the headwall to the pass. The other spurs visible below me also seemed to peter out before they got anywhere near a pass. The sightlines are improved by the extensive logging.

NAHATLATCH RIVER
Rating: 2–3

The Nahatlatch River does not waste time as it plunges out of the mountains towards the Fraser River. There is lots of white water on the river, but the several lakes (Frances, Hannack, and Nahatlatch) are very popular with canoeists. The road is mostly gravel, with one or two worn and rocky spots at the upper end. You will find good camping at several sites along the river, and a number of pull-outs by the lakes. The branch up Log Creek is currently the spur road used by loggers; when it's open, it leads to some important climbing areas.

GETTING THERE: Drive to Boston Bar and drop down to the river, crossing on the new bridge to North Bend. Follow the road north (right) for 16.0 km to the bridge over the Nahatlatch, and continue to the next fork. Go left (0 km).

DESCRIPTION: Stay left, ignoring the road and horse trail leading up the mountain. Pass Fir Flat campsite at 5.0 km. Cross a creek at 7.5 km and another campsite at 9.0 km.

The turn-off (right) to Log Creek is found at 10.0 km. The Log Creek Road may be followed nearly to the head of the valley, where there is active logging.

Farther up the Nahatlatch, at 10.5 km, is the turn-off to the Kookipi Creek Road.

At 11.0 km the Frances Lake campsite and several pull-outs beyond are suitable for one or two trucks. The old

Forest Service cabin is at 14.0 km. Several private cabins are located a short distance along the road. Nahatlatch Lake is at 15.6 km. There are several more campsites and a campground turn-off at 17.3 km. Cross a creek at 21.0 km and start climbing along the side of the mountain. This stretch is usually the roughest, and certainly quite jolting. Good views are a compensation. Cross a creek at 23.0 km and stay right twice. I stopped at the old trapper's cabin a few hundred yards beyond this point.

KOOKIPI–HARRISON LAKE TRAVERSE
Rating: 1–2

The most satisfying trips often involve crossing the countryside and not having to go back the same way one came. The nature of logging and the administration of our forests generally preclude routes that cross from one watershed to another. The Kookipi–Harrison traverse is an exception. This brand-new logging road starts from the Nahatlatch River near the Fraser Canyon, crosses the mountains, and then drops down along Big Silver Creek to Harrison Lake. The road passes through a thick tangle of old-growth forest destined to be harvested in the near future. The road presents few difficulties, and four-wheelers hope it will remain accessible.

GETTING THERE: From North Bend drive north for approximately 16 km to the bridge over the Natatlatch, continue to the next fork and take the left. Follow the Nahatlatch road for 10.4 km past the Log Creek turn-off. Turn left across the Kookipi (0 km).

DESCRIPTION: The road follows Kookipi Creek on a recently rehabilitated road, eventually leaving the second-growth timber and climbing into older, denser forest. Gradually the creek sinks into the valley as the road climbs to a pass at 30.0 km. There are long views of Mount Breakenridge in the distance.

The road now descends into the old cuts of the Big Silver Creek Valley. At 38.0 km stay left on the main road. At 41.3 km come to a T-intersection and stay left and downhill.

A spectacular new bridge has been built over an equally spectacular gorge at 50.0 km. At 52.1 km enter and then exit the G & F Logging Camp.

At 54.8 km stay left. The road now becomes the familiar east side road north of Harrison Lake. The total distance from the start of the route to the beaches and hot dog stands at Harrison is 95 km.

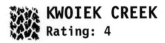 KWOIEK CREEK
Rating: 4

Kwoiek Creek rushes furiously over granite boulders and fallen trees from five placid high-altitude lakes. Kwoiek Lake is the most accessible, since the road runs along beside it and there are several small campsites. Kokwasakey Lake is hidden in the trees, but there is a trail to it. The logging road runs between the two upper lakes, John George and Klept, with tiny Kha Lake still higher. It will require some bushwhacking to get to the shorelines. There is, or used to be, a faint trail leading along the ridge between the Kwoiek and North Kwoiek Creeks to a small bump and a fine view of Antimony Mountain.

The Kwoiek road is rapidly deteriorating. Some sections are being washed bare, others beginning to unravel at the edges. The number of ditches forces drivers to move slowly and with care. Some good samaritan has marked the more dangerous holes with surveyor's tape.

GETTING THERE: Cross the bridge from Boston Bar to North Bend and turn left. Follow the West Side Road to 14 km, where it crosses the Nahatlatch River. At 15 km there is a fork. The road sharply left leads to Reo Rafting Tours, the road in the middle continues up the Nahatlatch, and the road sharply right and uphill leads up the West Side Road. Stay right.

At 22 km the road becomes rougher where it begins to follow the Hydro lines. At 32 km there is a fork. The right branch continues up the Fraser Canyon for about 14 km to the reaction ferry at Lytton. The left branch (0 km) is Kwoiek Creek.

DESCRIPTION: The Kwoiek road is not currently an active logging road and has begun to deteriorate. At 2 km cross a bridge. At 11 km cross a bridge and stay left or downhill at the fork. At 13 km there is a turn-off on the left to the end of Kwoiek Lake.

At 13.2 km a branch goes off to the right. This trail leads up the North Kwoiek Creek. About .3 km along this road it should be possible to hike onto a ridge that ascends gently to timberline and impressive views. However I stayed left on the main line.

I passed several possible campsites on this section, and a side road coming in from the left at 17 km. At 21 km there is a hiking trail sign on the left.

At 22 km the road crosses a bridge, heads for the other side of the valley and then begins to climb along the flank of the mountain. At 23 km I got a good glimpse of the lakes

Kwoiek Creek

and valley below. The road then descends the slope and crosses Kwoiek Creek once more between John George and Klept Lakes. Someone was camped at this bridge.

The road now follows the north side of the valley but ends at approximately 30 km. There is a good view from this old log dump and I almost considered camping here. A strong evening wind made me reconsider, and I retreated to the lower and warmer valley.

ANDERSON AND EAST ANDERSON RIVER
Rating: 1–4

The forest industry is spending millions of dollars trying to convince us of their sensitivity, responsibility and receptivity to public concerns. Actions, however, speak louder than words.

The two prime Catermole Timber logging roads, East Main and North Main, lead into some particularly exciting alpine country between the Fraser River and the Coquihalla. This "little Switzerland" of obscurely named granite peaks (Gemse, Reh, Serna, Gamuza, Zupjok) should be easily accessible by four-wheelers. Much to my dismay, when I returned to this area in 1990, I found the main access road blocked by a new logging camp. The new camp, surrounded by chain-link fencing, squats on the road several kilometres below the old logging camp and effectively blocks access to both East and North Main. Access for climbers, hikers, photographers and four-wheelers has become problematic. The routes remain in this guide in hopes that visitors may be able to contact Catermole Timber and obtain passage through this unfortunate obstacle.

GETTING THERE: Drive 40.0 km north from Hope up the Fraser Canyon (18.0 km past Yale), and over the Alexandra Bridge. Continue past the picnic area on Highway 1 for a hundred yards, and turn right on the Catermole logging road (0 km).

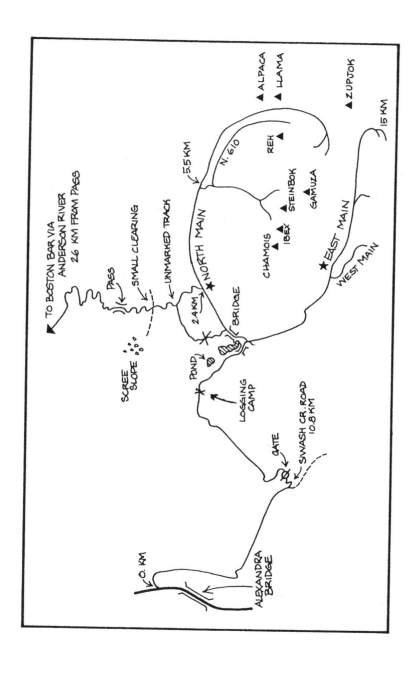

DESCRIPTION: A good, well-used, gravel logging road angles uphill. Stay right at 2.8 km, cross under the power lines at 5.0 km, and stay left past White's Road at 5.6 km.

The road makes a couple of switchbacks at 7.0 km and comes to a fork at 10.8 km. The right fork to Siwash Creek is being actively logged and is usually gated. Stay left and pass through the gate.

After zigzagging around the mountainside, come to the crest of the hill and the new logging camp at approximately 13.2 km. If you are unable to get through the camp, the road passes a small pond and a green lake before reaching the old campsite at 17.0 km.

From the camp you have four choices: linger at the camp exploring the old sheds and bunkhouses; take the easy (Class 1) East Main logging road, which heads south and east to the headwall beneath Zupjok Peak; take the rougher (Class 4) North Main road, which provides stunning views of the area's granite slabs and sharp summits; or try to find the fabled connection between the Anderson River watershed and the headwaters of East Anderson River.

East Main: Pass the logging camp turn-off (0 km), go right, climb to the top of the hill at 1.7 km, and then descend, crossing a bridge at 3.5 km.

The road now follows the north side of Anderson River. Stay left at 4.4 km and 10.0 km (although both forks may be worth exploring), following the road until it curves around the head of the valley and halts at approximately 15.0 km.

As you travel along the East Main road, the major peaks are to your left, with the eastern and southern ridges being less spectacular but no less rocky.

North Main: From the logging camp turn-off (0 km) stay left, cross a bridge and go right.

At .5 km stay right at the fork. (The left road goes up to logging patches and then returns to the North Main road about 2.0 km farther ahead). At 2.4 km stay right, following the North Main signs.

At 5.5 km a branch road (North 610) drops down to the river valley, crosses it at a ford (two large boulders limit the crossing to small trucks), and heads into the bowl beneath Chamois, Ibex and Steinbok peaks (from west to east respectively). There is a further branch on the south side of the river (North 600), which parallels the North Main road.

North Main now curves steadily south. The flagrantly improbable peak with the overhanging rock block is Reh Peak; the graceful sugarloaf behind it is Gemse. To the east the summits are Alpaca and Llama, which straddle the headwaters of Coldwater Creek above Coquihalla Lake.

The upper sections of North Main are cut by several washouts, which will generally get worse over time. We were stopped at 11.2 km by a particularly serious one—although a little digging and a chainsaw would probably make it passable (another washout is found a little farther on).

Anderson to East Anderson Traverse: The story goes that loggers far up the East Anderson realized that it would be considerably faster to haul logs out to the south, exiting near Alexandra Bridge, than it would be to go all the way north to Boston Bar. Accordingly, they pushed a track over the divide, only to run afoul of the Ministry of Forests, which promptly forced them to abandon this shortcut.

From the logging camp described above (0 km), take the North Main road. Crossing a bridge, go right at the intersection for 2.4 km, then turn left and uphill onto a side road.

This side road climbs a hill and starts to loop back down to North Main. Shortly before the road reaches the crest of the hill, however, a very faint and overgrown track strikes out to the right. This track heads uphill and zigzags to the left (appearing to approach a scree slope high on the ridge), cutting through a small clearing.

From the clearing the main track continues to the left, but an even more invisible and overgrown track goes right. Take this.

This overgrown path heads towards a break in the ridge. Just before the final approach there is an earth barrier to be crossed, and a steep rocky path. At the top, the path connects with a vast series of logging roads in the East Anderson River watershed. The distance from the turn-off to the pass is approximately 3.2 km.

The logging roads wind down the valley past Uztlius Creek and the Spius Creek intersection, and join Highway 1 just south of Boston Bar. (It is about 39 km from the pass to the highway.)

 ## UZTLIUS CREEK TRAVERSE
Rating: 3–4

Over the years, Uztlius Creek has become a standard weekend off-road trip. Many fourwheelers heading for the Merritt area get limbered up on this collection of old logging roads that follow the Anderson River, Uztlius Creek, and eventually Spius Creek to the Coquihalla Highway south of Merritt. Since the roads cross the spine of the Cascade Mountains through "old fashioned" clear cut, the views are often good.

Old timers, like Dan Bott, pronounce the name "Useless Creek." I was able to track down the origin of this malapropism. Years ago, loggers established a camp near the headwaters of the creek and cut timber ten or twelve hours a day, seven days a week for months without getting back to the relative civilization of Boston Bar. Working with handsaws and axes was a good way to work up a sweat, the grub was lousy (mostly beans), and the accommodations grim. The more fastidious loggers took a bath in the creek every four or five weeks.

The way I heard it, a young biologist was working his way up the creek, checking on the local fish population. He wasn't having much luck until he rounded a bend in the creek and, to his astonishment, came across about a dozen trout flopping around on the dusty bank. "What the heck's going on?" he said. The biggest of the trout rolled over and said bitterly, "Them loggers is taking their bath and the water in this stream stinks so bad it's just plain Useless."

Uztlius Creek Road

109

GETTING THERE: Gas up in Boston Bar and drive south for 2.1 km, taking the Uztlius Creek Forest Road to the left. Follow this steep gravel road for 5.5 km, keeping an eye out for logging trucks. Come to a fork in the road. The road left is marked "Uztlius/Stoyoma Forest Road." The road right is marked "Uztlius Creek Forest Road," and this is the start of the trail (0 km).

DESCRIPTION: Follow the road for 8 km, cross a bridge, and at 9.3 km pause to peer down into the Anderson River valley below. At 12 km the trail starts winding downhill. At 12.9 km a sign notes the Anderson Forest Road to the right. Stay left.

At 15 km cross a bridge and come to another fork. The Uztlius/East Anderson Road appears to be the main branch and heads up the hill to the right, eventually connecting with the Catermole operations mentioned elsewhere in this book. The less travelled road—to the left and sharply uphill—is the Uztlius Creek road.

Follow the Uztlius Creek road upward, then over several small bridges and a good-sized one at 18 km. Cross more bridges and stay left at a slash pile at 25.2 km. There is another bridge at 30 km, and a fork at 30.2 km. Stay right here, although it is the lesser used road.

At 33 km approach to a fork and a sign marking the end of the Uztlius Creek Road. Stay right, heading up a wide upper bowl, staying right again at 35.5 km. The road now begins a wide loop around the head of the valley, eventually dropping down to a shallow col and through the trees.

At 38 km stay left as a trail joins from the right. At 40 km stay left at a T-intersection, and pass a pond about two kilometers farther on. At 43 km the road swings to the left under the power line and begins to descend into the Spius Creek watershed.

You will start noticing old logging signs, i.e. "31 km," although the highway is actually a bit farther. Pass a turn-off to the left leading to a bridge across the creek, but take the next bridge a few hundred feet farther. Cross bridges near the 29 km and 24 km markers, and stay straight across a cattleguard and bridge shortly thereafter.

The road becomes a shelf road, passes a ranch and a sign noting that this is the Spius Creek Road at the 10 km marker. It then crosses the river 7 km farther on, and joins the highway at Patchett Road. Stay right and it will take you to Kingvale in about eight kilometers. Go left and under the railway tracks, then onto the Coquihalla Highway.

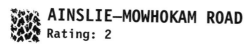 **AINSLIE–MOWHOKAM ROAD**
Rating: 2

The Ainslie/Mowhokam Forest Road leaves the Fraser Canyon and diagonally bypasses Lytton before joining Highway 1 along the Thompson River, south of Spences Bridge. Mostly, it passes through great clearcuts where the trees were cut in the early spring before the snow had melted. This accounts for the high stumps.

GETTING THERE: Follow Highway 1 north past Boston Bar for about 9 km to the Ainslie Creek Forest Road on the right (0 km). Alternatively, you may continue on up Highway 1 to just before the small airfield and the Blue Lake turn-off. If you take this road, turn off the highway, take a left fork, then a nondescript sandy fork to the right. Follow the right fork for about 2 km to a gate, then join the Ainslie Creek Road.

DESCRIPTION: The Ainslie Creek Road heads north for about 10 km before branching left to the North Ainslie Forest Road. Take this road. Stay left as two other roads join in over the next ten km.

At approximately 33 km pass a lake on the right, and start downhill. Come to a stump farm at 37 km and stay left, starting down the valley. The road now goes along the side of a ridge, crossing a stream at 44 km by an old shack. Travel along the right and come to a T-intersection. Stay left.

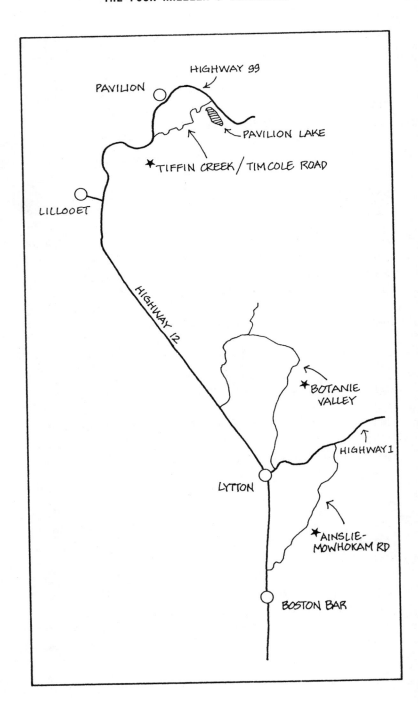

Pass through the Reserve, and onto the highway at 51 km.

BOTANIE VALLEY
Rating: 2

The ideal time to explore the Botanie Valley is during the first weeks of summer when the wildflowers are in bloom. The road climbs from the dry heat of Lytton into a beautiful valley, where expansive meadows are favoured by the most colourful and delicate of blossoms. Some of the side trails lead to higher elevations and gorgeous meadows.

Most weekenders travel up the Botanie Valley, then loop down to the Izman Road which brings one back to Highway 12 north of Lytton. However, those with more time can head towards either the Hat Creek Valley and Blue Earth Lake, or the Murray Creek Road that exits on Highway 1 near Spences Bridge.

GETTING THERE: Drive through Lytton, over the metal bridge, and .5 km to a junction. Take the paved road to the right (0 km).

DESCRIPTION: The road climbs steeply high above the narrow canyon of Botanie Creek. Passengers might watch for mountain sheep on either side of the road. Soon the road begins to level out, entering the valley floor, where there are numerous cabins, small ranches, and meadows. A few weathered old barns are always good for a scenic photograph on a sunny day.

The pavement ends at 11 km and becomes a first class gravel road. At 15 km the road crosses, then re-crosses Botanie Creek. Pass Botanie Lake and a small campsite at 17 km, then go through a cattle guard. The road becomes much narrower. Early in the year it is common to encounter a few small puddles and some bumps in this section.

The trail approaches Pasulko Lake at 23 km (stay right) and meanders above the lake shore in the trees. At 24 km

Mountain sheep, Botanie Valley

Botanie Valley—meadow running

pass the Native Outdoor School road to the left. Continue on the main road past some swampy areas, and into a logged area where there are almost always a few shallow mud puddles.

Come to a junction at 33 km. The road to the right leads to the Murray Creek Road (6 km), which goes right and ends up near Spences Bridge. Continuing on this road there is a side road left at approximately 8 km, which climbs to a high knoll with lots of flowers (and is a perfect picnic site). Or one can continue to the Hat Creek/Blue Earth road. The road left from the junction eventually exits at Izman Creek.

After staying left at the junction, enjoy the beautiful open meadows (a popular place to camp). At 37 km the road begins to angle to the left and downhill, passing several cabins. At 40 km the road starts downhill more steeply and soon starts to switchback. This section is very steep, so have your low gears ready. The road joins the Highway at 42 km.

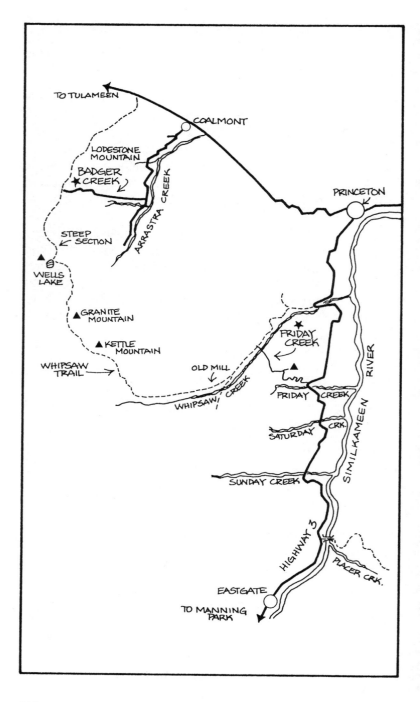

MANNING, SIMILKAMEEN, ASHNOLA

Highway 3 climbs out of Hope, enters Manning Provincial Park and then descends, making a long northerly curve through the town of Princeton and along the Similkameen River to Keremeos. The Allison Pass divide in Manning Park opens into visibly different country. The air becomes drier, the mountains relax into rolling hills, hemlock forest gives way to tightly clustered stands of lodgepole pine. At the lower elevations, the forest tapers off into arid hills and bounteous orchards. After the frequently cloudy skies and mossy brush of the coast, these can be welcome changes.

Four-wheelers have two choices. They may wish to explore the area north of Manning Park, generally described as the Whipsaw Area, or they may strike out to the east, into the vast area between Manning Park's Eastgate and Keremeos, generally described as the Placer Mountain Area.

The Placer Mountain Area is characterized by relatively low rolling hills, shared by loggers and cattlemen. To the north of the area is the Similkameen River, which rises in

Manning Park, flows north, then curves around and south to Keremeos. Highway 3 follows the river. On the south the region is bounded by the US border; on the east by the Ashnola River (a northeast flowing tributary of the Similkameen) and Cathedral Provincial Park. The town of Keremeos is an important source of the fruit we eat and the grapes for the wine we drink.

The Whipsaw Area is bounded by Manning Park on the south, the Similkameen and Highway 3 on the east and the Tulameen River (an east-flowing tributary of the Similkameen) on the north. The Whipsaw is criss-crossed by a number of historic trails: the Blackeye, Hudson Bay Brigade Trail, and Hope Pass. These were routes to the dreams of gold in the Cariboo, and the region is dotted with ghost towns and hollow mine shafts. In 1885, for example, Granite, near Arrastra Creek, looked like a potential metropolis. Fifteen years later it was gone.

The special nature of both areas demands special responsibilities from four-wheelers. In high summer the Placer Mountain Area is a tinder box, and even off-season this is a place for very small, Indian-style campfires—a few twigs make a warm flame and one spark can cause a large forest fire. This is also cattle country, and gates should be left as they are found. Drive carefully because there is very likely a cow just around the corner. Carry your own water since the streams are rather small.

The Whipsaw Area provides some of the worst evidence of irresponsible four-wheeling. If Jonathan Swift were to visit Wells Lake (the mid-point of the Whipsaw run), he would immediately recognize the leavings of "Yahoos," those brutes in human form who gave homo sapiens a bad name. Structures have been trashed, beer bottles heaved into the lake, every tree stabbed. The blame must rest with four-wheelers. On the other hand, there are campsites on Placer Mountain, visited only by four-wheelers, that are neat as a pin, not a bottle cap to be seen. Our reputation should rest on camps like these, and every four-wheeler who visits Wells Lake should do his/her bit to clean it up.

WHIPSAW
Rating: 7

The Whipsaw is a long, two-day trip with the hardest section right in the middle. Famous for its collection of mud puddles and tortuously winding trail, the Whipsaw also offers broad meadows, a placid lake and a challenging hill climb. No one should attempt this route without several companions and some trucks should be equipped with winches.

GETTING THERE: Drive through Manning Park and continue on Highway 3 towards Princeton. Pass Sunday and Friday Creeks and the mill opposite the Copper Mountain mine. The highway swings west and down into the cut of Whipsaw Creek. The road leaves the highway on the north side of the creek.

DESCRIPTION: The first 15–20 km are easy two-wheel driving. At 2.0 km, stay left. Stay right at 8.0 km. Pass the

Near the timberline at Whipsaw

Friday Creek exit at approximately 16.0 km. Stay right and uphill at the remains of a mill (17.0 km).

The road soon enters a freshly logged section where a bewildering variety of skid roads and spurs obscures the old main road. We had to search for the route, staying right at 19.0 km and then left .5 km beyond. Once you pass a small cabin, you will know you are on the right track.

The trail becomes a bit rougher and climbs towards the high country, passing the intersections with the Hope Pass and Dewdney trails (horses and hikers, not trucks). The Whipsaw trail climbs along the shoulder of Skaist and Kettle mountains, then drops down and climbs up the slopes of Granite Mountain. This section is heavily wooded and full of sharp corners, deep puddles and often remnants of winter snowdrifts. If the weather is wet—as it nearly always is—the travelling can become quite gruelling.

Once the trail skirts the summit of Granite Mountain, it begins to drop towards Wells Lake, which is approximately 40 km from the start. Negotiate the handmade bridge (reconstructed by locals after vandals destroyed it) and camp.

From Wells Lake, the trail continues north through the woods for 2 km before arriving at the base of the "Killer Hill." The Hill is the hardest single section of the trip and usually defeats one or two drivers in every party. The difficulties of the hill have been designed by nature and perfected by dozens of users. The soil has been scraped away, leaving a series of rocky shelves for the right side of the vehicle and loose rock for the left side. Each curve tends to nudge the vehicle to the edge, and attempts to correct it result in hanging up on the rocks. Those without limited slip will have the most difficulty.

Mercifully the going begins to ease up shortly beyond the hill. Pass the Brigade Trail at 7.0 km. Stop for lunch or a second campsite at Lodestone Lake at 12.0 km. Then proceed along the ridge until it begins to drop down from the mountain towards the Arrasta Creek junction at 28.0 km.

Dawn at Wells Lake

Stay left and head for Rice Road at 33.0 km, and turn left to reach Coalmont and Tulameen, or right to return to Princeton.

WHIPSAW VARIATION: FRIDAY CREEK
Rating: 6

Friday Creek is a variant approach to the popular Whipsaw, although it may be taken as a separate trip just as easily. A little moderate four-wheeling will get you to the top of a mountain and grant you a preview of the Whipsaw area. The descent from the head of Friday Creek is something different altogether: one of the narrowest, steepest tracks in this volume. So steep, in fact, that running in the lowest gears with the assistance of the brakes does not always seem enough. To make matters more challenging, the path is usually blocked by a lot of deadfall. A chainsaw in good running order, with lots of fuel, should not be forgotten.

GETTING THERE: Travel through Manning Park and north on Highway 3 as it follows the Similkameen River. Note that each major bend in the highway is for a creek, and that these creeks are named for days of the week: Sunday, Saturday and Friday. The Friday Creek Road (marked by a sign on the gate) leaves the highway at one of the larger, deeper bends. Turn left through the gate (0 km).

DESCRIPTION: The trail starts steeply and switchbacks upward, then levels off about a kilometre later. At 2.6 km you get a good glimpse of the highway below.

At 5.0 km the trail forks. You will take the left fork, but first try the right fork, which leads to a small summit with a vast view. After a break, retrace your path and head down into the trees.

At first the descent is relatively gentle, but by kilometre 7 it becomes much steeper—then much, much steeper. Be prepared to stop and scramble ahead through the bushes to clear away deadfall, and certainly try not to slip over the side. A mistake on this trail could require a lot of time-consuming correction.

By the time you have gone 12.0 km, the track levels out and curves left towards the main Whipsaw road—crossing a logged-off area and fording a small stream to get there. Your exit will be close to the 20 km sign of the Whipsaw.

From this point you can choose either to head right back to civilization (Highway 3 heading for Princeton) or go left to an abandoned ore mill and Whipsaw.

Note: The Whipsaw trip is a tough one, requiring good preparation for mud holes. After turning left onto a good logging/mining road, follow it to the abandoned ore mill, staying right at the first major intersection. After the mill, the road deteriorates. Stay right at the next two intersections and follow the track (staying on the track!) up over Skaist and Kettle mountains. Cross the Dewdney/Paradise horse trail and head down Granite Mountain to Wells Lake.

This is the usual camping spot. From the lake you may return as you came, driving past the Friday Creek turn-off to the highway, a few kilometres south of Princeton.

AGATE MOUNTAIN
Rating: 4–5

Travel through time and your own childhood fantasies on this backcountry trip. Leave the hustle of the tourist route from Princeton to Keremeos, and make a cross-country detour through an old but working ranch, up a valley right out of one of those Saturday matinee westerns. Then (after some four-wheeling) visit an isolated Fire Watch with a terrific view of thousands of acres of forest, and pass by a mountaintop bit of high technology, before making an easy

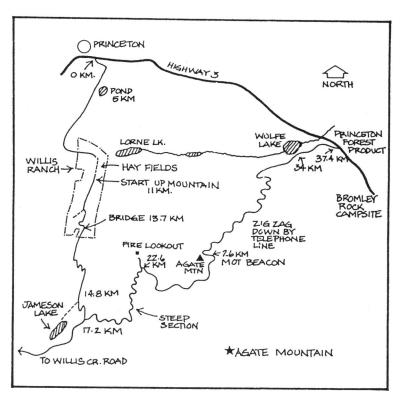

descent back to Highway 3 and continuing to the fruit stands of Keremeos.

GETTING THERE: From Princeton drive east along Highway 3 to the Princeton campsite sign (left) or the weathered Amber Ski Hill sign (right), and turn right up a good paved road (0 km) through the local golf course and onto a well-cared-for gravel road.

DESCRIPTION: Continue from 0 km over hill and dale, in two-wheel drive, past a pond on your left (5.0 km) and through a Private Property sign (8.0 km) marking the boundary of the old Willis Ranch. It may be a good idea to call ahead from Princeton to tell them you are coming— and simply passing through.

Continue along the ranch road to 9.2 km and a fork. The right branch leads to the ranch buildings: several houses, a trailer, picnic table, barns, etc. If you did not ask permission previously, I would recommend you do so now.

The left branch leads to—and around—the hayfields, and beyond to Lorne Lake (and the valley through which you will eventually exit). However, your task is to make your way through the fields (avoiding the irrigation equipment) to the right (south). Aim for a road that leads between a curious, treed "dunce cap" and the mountainside to the right.

At 11.0 km the road leaves the fields and starts up the mountainside, following a large, iron irrigation pipe. There is a gate on the hillside at 12.5 km.

Once again come to a fork. The right fork leads down into the ranchers' upper fields, so take the left around the side and across a small bridge (13.7 km). Cross the bridge and go right, starting your ascent.

Now you are ascending the mountainside, weaving in and out around the bluffs. The forest opens up again above the end of the fields, and the trail becomes rougher.

There is another fork at 14.8 km. The right branch (down a switchback) heads towards a dead end at Jameson Lake (washed-out stream, bushes and a brown bear cub—I did not stick around long enough to find the mother). The left heads uphill. Follow this shelf road to another intersection at 17.2 km. The right fork presumably links up with the Willis Creek main line and wanders back to Copper Mound to the west. The left fork heads towards Agate Mountain.

The switchbacks begin in earnest, each one a little steeper than the last. There are approximately 3.0 km of four-wheeling like this.

At 22.6 km a side road (left) leads to the fire lookout station. A good, old-fashioned fire lookout has something nautical about it—it is neatly kept and organized like a ship. Instruments, radio, bunkbed, table, stove, desk. The view from the lookout (which overlooks Willis Ranch) is marvellous. Much of the timber has not been cut recently, and shaggy green hills extend in every direction. However, the warden remembers the big fires of a decade ago, when thousands of acres burned.

Having checked out the fire lookout, go back down to the road and continue into the forest. Pass through a gate at 23.0 km and then climb to the Ministry of Transport beacon at 26.0 km. This high-tech operation hums with air conditioners, and is protected by forbidding signs and a lot of cow dung.

From here, simply drive down the mountainside via innumerable switchbacks (following the telephone poles), while carefully trying to avoid the cattle. At 34.0 km pass Wolfe Lake on your left, and exit through a Forest Service gate at 37.4 km, back onto Highway 3 (just west of Princeton Forest Products mill).

Clearly this is not a shortcut, but the trip is a welcome change after miles of highway driving.

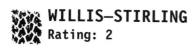
WILLIS–STIRLING
Rating: 2

The system of roads I call Willis–Stirling bypass the highway between Princeton and Hedley by circling around

Agate Mountain. No one will save much time by taking this shortcut along a series of logging roads through the thick lodgepole pine forests of the Wilbert Hills. The road exits not far from Hedley. Early in the season travellers may encounter snow, although by mid-summer the soft roadbed may be pretty dusty.

GETTING THERE: From Princeton go east across the bridge, then turn right on the Copper Mountain Road (0 km).

DESCRIPTION: Copper Mountain Road is paved and winds uphill for several kilometers, passing the Corsi Ranch at 9 km and then dropping downhill for a couple of km before climbing again.

At 15 km come to a junction. The paved road continues right to the mine, while a gravel road goes left. This is the Willis Creek Road.

The Willis Creek Road twists and turns. At 19 km we passed a tiny side road on the left. It may be that this path connects with the Agate Mountain system, but in April it was clogged with snow so we did not try it. We continued on the main road, crossing the creek at 20.4 km.

At 21.7 we noticed that the spur roads began to have names. The road to the right was signed, "Commander," but we ignored this imperative and stayed left and uphill. Similarly at 23 km we ignored "Nichols" and stayed right.

We crossed a stream, went through a fence and at 30 km ignored a side road to the left. We crossed another creek at 38 km, passed over a cattleguard at 41 km, and another one 4 km farther.

From this point it was an easy 7 km to the highway. The road exits across from the Stirling Creek Ranch, a few km west of the Corona Store.

PLACER LAKE
Rating: 6

Some philosophers argue that suffering must precede enjoyment. The lake is a beautiful spot, a fine place to watch a fly fisherman cast a golden thread through the early evening light towards circular ripples. But one does not reach this idyllic and secluded mountain lake without some suffering, as the thick coating of black rubber on the boulders of the last stretch indicates. One can read on the rocks the frustration and determination that preceded the final achievement.

GETTING THERE: Cross Manning Park on Highway 3, and continue on past the Eastgate Esso station to the turn-off (right) in the middle of a switchback by Copper Creek campsite. This is approximately 24.0 km from the Manning Park Lodge, 19.0 km from Eastgate (0 km).

DESCRIPTION: Cross the bridge, pass the Weyerhaeuser warning sign and head up a good gravel forestry road, staying left on the main line and up three switchbacks. Avoid a couple of side paths, and cross a creek bed at 2.5 km.

Continue upwards through the dry, dusty hills, around one ridge and up another to 9.3 km. Branch right off the Placer Mountain Road, and descend the ridge.

At 11.3 km there is a junction. Either road will work. The right road curves downhill past a corral, crosses the stream and then heads left to a wranglers' parking lot and up to a road. Go right.

The left fork gets you to the same spot, just beyond the wranglers' camp, via a crossing of Watson Creek and a couple of curves above the camp. The road drops down and meets the lower road.

After the upper and lower forks have rejoined, the track becomes bumpy, muddy and sometimes dusty. There is another fork less than 1 km later. The left fork leads to a log patch. The right fork, near a blue rock, squeaks between two trees and then curves left. This is the hard part.

The last couple of kilometres to the lake are Class 6. The trail tends to curve to the right, with the toughest and steepest being the first section. It looks like more than one four-wheeler has failed here. Once the trail turns left, however, the rest is easy, and the lake is only a few hundred metres away.

There is a limited number of campsites on the lake.

PLACER MOUNTAIN–ASHNOLA TRAVERSE
Rating: 4–5

This traverse, or shortcut, from Manning Park to Cathedral Park is not so difficult but rather tricky. In several spots it is easy to get off the track. The logging roads through the extensively cut areas are a mixture of old and new, and the mountainous terrain is not distinct enough to allow drivers to aim for some distant point and go to it. The search for a way through is part of the fun.

Placer Mountain is dry country and gets drier as you go east towards the Ashnola River, so special care should be taken with fires. The chief pleasure of the route is the middle section, which is an old winding path through relatively mature forest; it sure would not be much fun if it were charred stumps.

GETTING THERE: Pass through Manning Park and Eastgate (the last gas before Keremeos), drive down to the Copper Creek campsite turn-off (19.0 km from Eastgate), and turn right (0 km).

DESCRIPTION: Take the forestry road (used by Weyerhaeuser, as the sign states) for 9.3 km as it winds and switchbacks up and around two ridges, before coming to a major fork and a good viewpoint.

Take the left fork (the right leads to Placer Lake) and

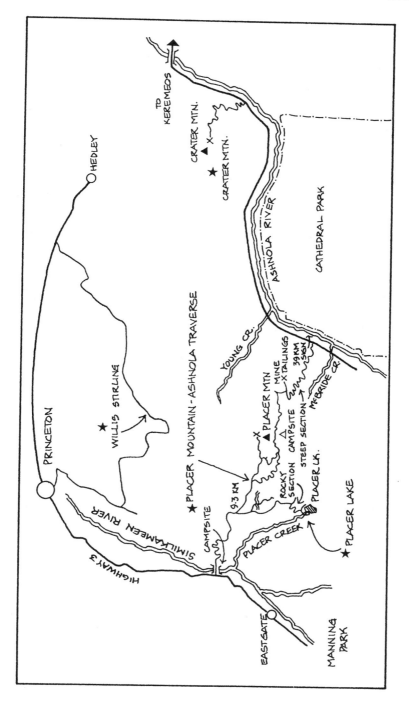

Placer Mountain

Descending Placer Mountain

follow a rolling ridge below the crest. About halfway along, a track drops down to the right and into the bushes. This track connects with the tiny forest track that edges around Placer Mountain. (*Note:* It is also possible to continue below the ridge towards the low point and branch off higher up, taking a tiny trail to the right. This track also connects with the trail around Placer Mountain.)

The trail winds through the forest, passing a beautiful little campsite with a fine view, and a small stream about 1 km farther along the road. A spur road also goes left to just beneath the rocky summit of the mountain.

A few kilometres distant, the road comes to an intersection. Take the road right and downhill. This is the start of the steep section—a series of very tight switchbacks—which means low gears. Those who have larger trucks or who are slower at the steering wheel, will need to back up to get around these corners. The first two switchbacks are over sharp red rock, the next two over blocky ochre and the last two are plain, old-fashioned dirt. (If you are coming up from the Ashnola, red rock is a sign that you are almost at the top.)

The road continues to snake down the mountain and eventually reaches the Ashnola Road at 35 km. Stop and think before roaring onto the Ashnola Road. The logging trucks really barrel along this stretch and the drivers do not expect to see four-wheelers wandering out of the bush. Turn left and pass several campsites on the way into the highway outside Keremeos.

Note: If you are travelling from the Ashnola towards Manning Park, the start of the trail may be hard to find. Turn off up the Ashnola River Road (there's a sign for the lodge at Cathedral Park), cross the beautiful, covered red bridge and pass through the reserve and up the valley past the various campsites (the last is Buckhorn). Look for the forest company mileage sign reading 39. The Placer Mountain trail is the next right. It is not marked, but if you look up it you will see a large broken tree trunk in front of a slash pile. This is the right road.

CRATER MOUNTAIN
Rating: 3

Humans are never satisfied. We flee the damp, dismal coast in order to find dry air and hot sunshine. Having camped along the Ashnola River south of Keremeos for a couple of days, I was tired of the oppressive heat and the dust of rumbling logging trucks. So I headed up Crater Mountain in hopes of finding some median between cool rainforest and the dry vineyards and orchards of the Similkameen. The weather on top (1000 metres up) was cooler, but still on the warm side.

Several kilometres from the end of the road (a shoulder of Crater Mountain), I realized that I was following a young fellow on a mountain bike. He pedalled furiously while my CJ7 chugged relentlessly behind him. I stopped several times, hoping to take the pressure off. We met on top and shared suggestions for other places to visit. On the way down I caught up with him again, but only because he had crashed and broken his hand trying to round a rocky curve.

GETTING THERE: Drive northwest out of Keremeos on Highway 3 to the turn-off (south) onto the Ashnola River Road. Cross the covered bridge, pass through the Indian Reserve and into the Ashnola Valley. There are several campsites upriver—all of them subject to dust from the road—but the best is Buckhorn. The turn-off to Crater Mountain comes sooner: 9.0 km from the turn-off from Highway 3, just after crossing the river, find a dirt road leading off and up to the right (0 km).

DESCRIPTION: The road, which zigzags up a ridge beside Red Bridge Creek, immediately starts to switchback.

Cross a small stream (3.7 km) and cool off. (However, since cattle are grazing above, I used the shade and not the water for this purpose.)

Stay left at 4.6 km and left again at 5.8 km. (The latter

track, however, may lead as close to the Red Bridge ponds—and their fishing—as it is possible to drive.)

At 12.2 km come to the crest of the ridge and a sign stating there is no motor travel beyond this point—an unnecessary sign because the road ends at the stream about a hundred metres beyond. I climbed to a grassy knoll and surveyed the countryside. To get a view of the Cathedral Park mountains it would have been necessary to spend another hour climbing to the summit of Crater Mountain. I preferred to sit where I was and watch the breeze flatten the grass.

I let the CJ make her own way down in low range—being reluctant to get to the hot floor of the valley in a hurry.

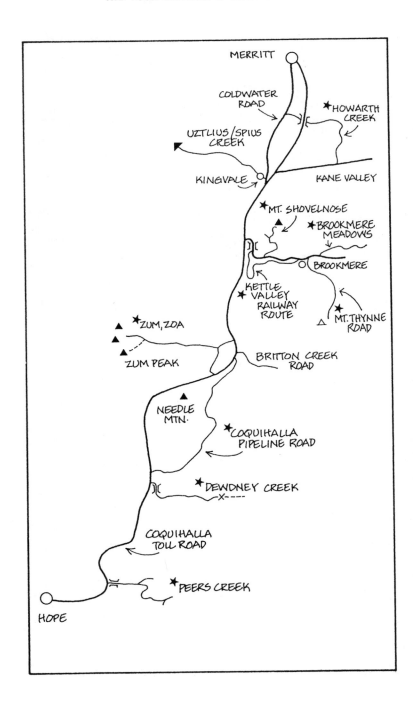

SECTION EIGHT
COQUIHALLA

Thanks to the Coquihalla Toll Road, the traffic jam that forms at the Cassiar Connector on summer weekends begins to break up somewhere south of Merritt. The Coquihalla has greatly expanded the cruising range of BC motorists, and probably contributed to the real estate boom in the Okanagan. Breezing along at 110 kph along this engineering feat, the traveller glimpses sheer granite monoliths, forested hills and working ranches, all for a $10 fee.

This is an area rich in history. A pack trail to the Fraser was constructed up Boston Bar Creek in 1860 for miners during the gold rush. The ill-starred Kettle Valley Railway branched near Brookmere and crept south along the steep slopes of the Coquihalla River. Avalanches and rockfalls continually threatened the railway, and ultimately resulted in its closing. The Coquihalla Highway circumvents the worst section of the old railway route when it bypasses Needle Mountain to the west before climbing to the Coquihalla summit.

Twenty years ago, the Coquihalla River was a favourite

four-wheel drive playground. The early four-wheel drive clubs from Surrey took dozens of old Internationals, CJ5s, and the original Broncos up the twisting pathway along the river for weekend outings. They sometimes met residents of Merritt trying to get down to Hope to do some shopping.

Many of the side roads off the Coquihalla are blocked, but several allow us to sample the alpine terrain, get a glimpse at historic pathways, or meander leisurely through the meadows and pastures of the Interior.

PEERS CREEK
Rating: 2

According to the maps, the headwall of Peers Creek is the start of a pack trail that crosses the Hozameen Mountains to Tulameen. Hikers, however, might want to attempt to hoof it from the end of this logging road to the ridges on the south which overlook the Nicolum Creek valley.

Peers Creek

GETTING THERE: Join the highway at Hope, take a couple of bends and exit at the Kawkawa Exit, stay right and cross the bridge (0 km).

DESCRIPTION: The trail joins the creek and crosses a small stream at 1 km. At 1.5 cross a bridge and begin to climb. This section is fairly steep.

Stay right at 3.4 km, and again at 4.7 km. At 5 km we crossed the bridge and went right. The road to the left leads to recent logging, and also the pack trail (if it still exists).

At 5.7 keep to the right, and start uphill again. Watch out for the rather deep ditch at 6.1 km. After surmounting this ditch, take note of the waterfall on the right, then switchback upwards at 7.2 km.

At 8.2 we stayed right, but at 9 km we chose to go left. The right road seems to angle across the slope towards the westernmost shoulder. It should be easy to bushwhack up to the ridge from this road.

The left fork ends at a log dump site at 10 km. It should also be possible to hike up to the ridgeline from this point. The mountain down the valley is Ogilvie Peak, which stands between the confluence of the Coquihalla River and the Fraser River.

DEWDNEY CREEK
Rating: 1

The Dewdney Creek road deserves further exploration. I confess that when confronted with an obstacle, I choose discretion over valour and retreated. My excuses included the fact that I was alone, my tires were old and worn, and I figured that it would take a lot of earth-moving to get me unstuck. A small landslide had covered an uphill section of the road with a mixture of sand and rocks bigger than softballs but smaller than basketballs.

I stopped, walked over the patch, moved a few rocks, picked my route, put the truck in its lowest gear and jerked forward. I went about twenty feet before the rear wheel started digging in and the front end started to slide a little towards the edge of the precipice. I made a second attempt, and the same thing happened. At this point, reason told me that sooner or later I would be dug in up to my frame and be forced to dig myself out. Wishful thinking told me that a larger party could have done a little engineering, or used one of the heavier, more powerful trucks to clamber over the section and tug the rest of us up. The road ahead looked in good shape, but any attempt to cross this slide in its present condition greatly increases the difficulty of this route.

GETTING THERE: Drive up the Coquihalla and take the Carolin Mines Road Exit. Go east, cross the Bailey bridge and go right (0 km).

DESCRIPTION: After crossing the bridge, follow the road uphill along the creek. It appears that a major flood has torn up the creekbed recently.

At 5 km cross a bridge. Note the old ford to the right and the small campsite.

At 5.6 km I took notice of a magnificent old cedar, a reminder of the forests of yore. At 5.8 km I stayed straight and bypassed a bridge and a trail going off to the right. This trail seems to go high onto the shoulder of the mountain and might be worth exploring.

At 7 km was halted by a slide across the road. I walked a little ways up the road beyond the slide, and it seemed fine.

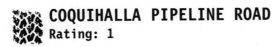 **COQUIHALLA PIPELINE ROAD**
Rating: 1

This side road, sometimes known as "Portia's shortcut," takes longer than the Coquihalla highway, but bypasses the steepest section of the highway by following a pipeline road and the old Kettle Valley railway bed to the east of Needle Mountain. Several old trestles and tunnels are in evidence,

Old Kettle Valley Railroad tunnel, Coquihalla Pipeline Road

and it is easy to see how this ultimately unrewarding attempt to run a railway through avalanche country cost so much blood, sweat and tears.

This road is generally in good shape, the greatest danger being an occasional deep pothole or a small boulder in the road. The sections of the road built over the old railway bed are narrow and the drop-off a little sheer, but this shouldn't deter four-wheelers with even the most modest experience of back roads.

GETTING THERE: Take the Coquihalla Highway north out of Hope and exit at Portia station. Go through the gate (0 km) marking the beginning of the pipeline road. If the gate is locked, return to the Coquihalla and try again at another time.

DESCRIPTION: Follow the pipeline road uphill and into the Coquihalla River valley. There are a number of small campsites along this section of the road. Pass a swampy area at 14 km. At 21 km there is a nice view of a trestle still standing high on the slope to the west. Cross the river and follow the slope until the track levels out and eventually rejoins the Coquihalla toll road near the toll booth at 24 km.

Note: The west side of the Portia exit has an historical marker describing the old Boston Bar pack trail. The current trail, however, just goes back to a fence by the highway.

ZUM, ZOA AND VICUNA
Rating: 5

This challenging trail almost had me scavenging in my storage room for my rock climbing shoes, Royal Robbins shorts, Patagonia shirt, rusty pitons, and worn nylon rope. Almost, but not quite. If I were half as old or twice as tough, or both, I might been tempted to go back to this valley with all my gear, but I am content to savour the visual memories of these oddly affecting granite thumbs with the curious names. Backpackers might consider hiking into Little Douglas Lake to spend a couple of nights surrounded by sheer rock slabs and a coverlet of bright stars.

GETTING THERE: Drive past the Zopkius Ridge outlook and take the Falls Lake turnoff, winding under the road and driving up to a clearing at the trailhead to Falls Lake (0 km).

(Alternatively, drive through the Toll Booth and take Exit 228, drive through the Highways maintenance facilities and find the sign reading Upper Coldwater Forest Road.)

DESCRIPTION: From the clearing, take the muddy, deteriorating track going up the hill to the right. Watch out for the deep ditch at 1 km before the road levels off. Be

Bare rock and stumps along the Zum, Zoa, Vicuna trail

Vicuna Mountain

careful again at 2.4 km where the trail climbs to the right, swings left over a bump, and then drops down sharply. The view up the valley is good from this point.

Follow a shelf road gradually downhill towards the valley. Parts of this road are becoming close to impassable. Come to an intersection at 4 km and take a left up the valley. (This is where those who started from Exit 228 will join the path, having crossed one bridge after the end of the paved road.)

The road winds up the valley. It is hard to pay much attention to the road because the view is so interesting. Pass a side road right that goes down to the creek. Cross a bridge at 6.1 km.

The Zum Peak Forest campsite is at 7.8 km, just before a bridge. It only has space for one or two trucks. A trail leading to Little Douglas Lake starts here (about 4 km on the map). Presumably Zoa Peak is on the left, and Zum Peak on the right.

The main road continues to bump along up the valley, winding in and out of the forest beside the Coldwater River. The peaks on the horizon are (left to right) Llama, Alpaca, Vicuna, and Guanaco. What is a Guanaco anyway?

At 12.6 km I stayed left, and crossed a bridge at 13.1 km. The road ends at a tree planters' camp at 13.4 km. Perhaps it was the altitude, but I thought the sheer grey granite overlooking the bleached stumps of the clearcut made for a thoroughly surrealistic scene.

KETTLE VALLEY RAILWAY LOOP
Rating: 1

This little quickie follows the Kettle Valley Railway on a ten kilometre loop from the Coldwater Exit into the town of Brookmere. I have heard two stories about how it came to be.

First, that the loop marks where the Kettle Valley line split, with the southern section following the Coquihalla canyon to the south. The other story is more plausible.

Railway buffs will tell you the Coquihalla section of the Kettle Valley railway was the worst. Engineers used to say their rosaries before starting down this section, because the odds were pretty good that an avalanche would sweep the whole train off the tracks and down the slopes into the river. The brakemen back in the caboose carried along a big three pronged grappling hook attached to a chain. When the avalanche hit the engine, the guys at the back would threw out the hook hoping to snag the cliff and hold the train from being swept down into the icy river below. One winter morning, a brakeman named Charlie accidently kicked the grappling hook off the back of the train shortly after they left Brookmere. He did not realize his mistake until the train seemed lose power about five kilometers down the canyon. He looked back, and darned if the hook hadn't snagged the track and dragged it into a big loop. It's been that way ever since.

GETTING THERE: Take the Coquihalla past the toll booth and take the Coldwater River exit. Stay right on the Coldwater Road, then take a right off the pavement onto a gravel road (0 km).

DESCRIPTION: Pass a shed at 1 km, cross two trestles at 6 kms, two more at 6.7, and another at 7.7. Cross the Coldwater at 8.6 km and start back towards Brookmere. At 9.2 km the railway bed begins to parallel the Brookmere road again. Pass through a meadow and a gate, rejoin the road and enter Brookmere.

SHOVELNOSE MOUNTAIN
Rating: 2

The summit of Shovelnose does not provide a memorable panorama, although you do get a good view of the Coquihalla Highway from an altitude of 1686 meters. The trail follows the telephone lines to a repeater station and is home to a large bovine population.

GETTING THERE: Pass the Larson Hill exit, then take the Coldwater River Exit and head towards Brookmere. Cross bridges at 1.5 km and again at 2.2 km. At 7.7 km look for an unmarked road angling off to the left (0 km).

DESCRIPTION: Start up the hill, which briefly becomes a shelf road and switchbacks sharply to the left. At 1.6 km it switchbacks again, this time to the right.

At 2.6 km the road switchbacks again to the left, crosses under the telephone lines and climbs to an open area on the shoulder. Be sure not to miss the faint track to the right, otherwise you will end up wandering around a maze of cattle paths on the slope of the mountain. Take this right track up the ridge, rather than the more travelled road which continues straight ahead.

The trail now follows the ridge line through meadows, forests and grazing cattle. At 3.6 km pass a collapsed telephone company shed. The angle of the road increases slightly and passes a side road at 5.3.

The road dips down briefly and then begins to climb again, entering into a a thicker forest. A fence appears on the right.

The summit, at 8 km, has two sharp switchbacks near the very top. The summit itself barely has enough room for two trucks and the various buildings related to the telephone equipment.

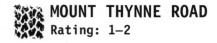 ## MOUNT THYNNE ROAD
Rating: 1–2

The view from Mount Thynne should be excellent, but the trip should be saved until mid-summer when the snow melts. We only got as far as Brook Lake, which looks like a (literally) cool place to camp. For our party, the nicest part of the trip was examining the beautiful old wooden water tower and caboose at Brookmere.

GETTING THERE: Leave the Coquihalla Toll Road at the

Coldwater Exit and drive east to the old railway town of Brookmere. Drive through the town past the water tower and take the marked Mount Thynne Road to the right (0 km).

DESCRIPTION: From the turn-off, drive 1.8 km and stay

The water tower at Brookmere

left. The right fork *may* be the road that reaches Brook Lake from the west. At 4.4 km stay right, and again at 6.4 km. Once again keep to the right at 10 km.

At 12 km a road branches off to Andy's Lake on the right. We stayed left and continued uphill. At 14.2 km we came to a junction. The road right follows the contour of the hill and dead-ends just over the ridge. A road just before the stream seems to head up into the basin, and perhaps onto the ridge leading to Mount Thynne. A road just to the west of the stream seems to do the same thing, and if the maps are correct, this road is the correct one.

BROOKMERE MEADOWS
Rating: Class 1

This is a gentle little pathway across forests and pasture. Even the most grizzled four-wheeler should be open to the possibility of enchantment. By enchantment, I mean the chance of being seduced away, however briefly, from thoughts of gears and engine rpms by the sheer beauty of a spring landscape. For hundreds of years travellers have paused to enjoy such sights. John Thomson in 1728, long before four-wheel drive, wrote: "Come gentle Spring, ethereal mildness come, and from the bosom of your dripping cloud...music wakes around...." If that is too rich, just enjoy the greenery.

GETTING THERE: From the Coquihalla Toll Road take the Coldwater River Exit. Drive through Brookmere to the Forest Road sign (0 km) and stay straight.

DESCRIPTION: Follow the Forest Road to the top of the hill (4.3 km), and past a meadow and an old barn (7.4 km). Ignore the side road at 8.2 km and go straight on. Pass the Colony Lakes road on your left at 8.8 km and look for birds nesting around the pond at 10.4 km.

A side road enters from the left at 10.7 and another at 12.7. Stay right and reach the Otter Creek Road at 13.7 km. Turn left, and pass Voght Road on the left.

At 15 km leave the main road and go right through more meadows and past another pond. Cross a cattleguard at 17 km, climb gently to a nice view of the mountains to the right, and enter more pastures. There is a wire gate at 20 km, and at 22 km the track is joined by the road from the ranch visible to the left. Cross the stream, pass a gravel pit, go through another gate and exit under the Pike Mountain Ranch sign at 24 km and onto Highway 5 shortly thereafter.

It is roughly 50 km to Merritt (north) and 37 km (south) to Princeton.

HOWARTH CREEK
Rating: 3

While bumping along Howarth Creek I discovered the answer to a philosophical question. One side of my brain was lamenting the fact that sticky soda pop had splashed out of the can held in the dashboard holder and gummed up the buttons on my radio. The other side of my brain realized why I like these obscure little side roads. The Coquihalla is the conquest of nature, a gigantic slash across the landscape that confounds any natural obstacles. In contrast, the Howarth Creek Road was built when men were more humble towards nature, and tended to give way to, or conform to, the curves and hillocks of the landscape. The thick forest, the bouquets of purple lupins in the sunlight, and the road itself seemed at peace with each other.

The Howarth Creek road begins south of Merritt on the old Coldwater Road, crosses under the Coquihalla, and then loops around south to join the Kane Valley Road and exit at Kingvale.

GETTING THERE: Follow the Coldwater Road south out of Merritt for about 6 or 8 km through the reserve and several ranches, until you see a side road marked Gwen Lake Road-Tolko 16. Turn left onto it (0 km).

Old cabin along the Howarth Creek trail

DESCRIPTION: Take the Gwen Lake Road uphill towards the Coquihalla, passing an abandoned ranch at 2 km, and taking the lighted tunnel under the Coquihalla at 4 km.

A good gravel road winds uphill, passing a side road coming in from the right at 5.9. I stayed right at 6.4 km, where a cabin is visible in a meadow to the right.

At the 9 km sign I stayed right. The road left may lead to Gwen Lake, which I never found, although I did pass a lily pond shortly thereafter.

At 10 km there are side roads both right and left, but I stayed straight ahead.

The fork at 12 km is crucial. Take the left fork. I spent an hour or two wandering aimlessly on Selish Mountain's logging roads because I went right.

At 13 km cross under the power lines. From this point on, I encountered small mudholes and dips of various degrees of difficulty.

There is a clearing at 14.3 km and I went straight uphill towards the right. I passed a pond at 16.4 km, stayed right at 16.7 km. There is a deep ditch here, drive slowly.

At 17.2 km there is a gate marking the Nicola Ranch property. Leave the gate as you found it. At 20 km the road ends at the Kane Valley Road. To return to the Coquihalla go right (about 11 km).

The Kane Valley Road follows a broad valley. The road to Boss Lake goes left at the 9 km marker. Once you cross back under the highway and a trestle, it is possible to go right back to Merritt (31 km), or left to the highway entrance (4 km) at Brookmere.

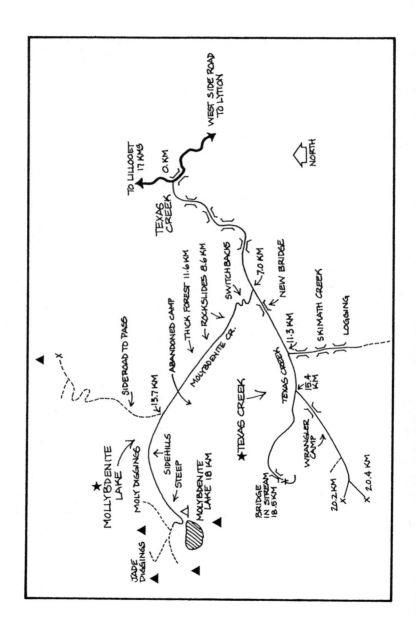

Section 8
LILLOOET AREA

The bustling hub of Lillooet takes us to the limits of those trails easily reached from Vancouver on a weekend, and marks the beginning of entirely new possibilities. For those travelling over the Duffey Lake Road or toiling up the Fraser Canyon, Lillooet signifies a welcome chance to feed, fuel up, and stretch one's legs. The town has several gas stations, restaurants, mechanics, an auto parts store and a District Forest Service office.

In 1860, Lillooet was a place to rest and obtain provisions after travelling the Douglas Trail from the coast, and the place to prepare for a journey along the Cariboo Trail to Clinton and the Cariboo. Today, it offers the back road explorer the rewards of stunning scenery and serious four-wheeling in every direction: towards Carpenter Lake and the Yalakom River, along the banks of the Fraser, or up the Caribou Highway toward Pavilion and Clinton.

The terrain and climate are surprisingly varied. The Fraser flows through dry country. The trails along the benches above the river have a fine sandy soil that is dusty in the sunshine, but becomes an awful, slippery mud when wet. The roads leading inland rise through several forest zones, each one with smaller trees, until it merges with wet meadows, burbling streams and millions of flowers. At timberline the size of the plants diminishes to tiny, perfect alpine flowers, while the sky seems to blossom into a huge canvas for billowing white clouds. The days may be blistering hot, while the nights are often cold and windy.

TEXAS CREEK–MOLYBDENITE LAKE
Rating: 5–6

The network of roads in the Texas Creek area south of Lillooet leads to some of the most beautiful alpine and meadow areas of southwestern British Columbia. They are places to spend a weekend or a week, and they are the trailhead for a long backpack. Molybdenite Lake will be of particular interest to rockhounds. One walking path from the lake leads to abandoned molybdenum diggings, another to much older jade mines, and a nearby ridge is reputed to hide a rich vein of silver. Sun worshippers will find the weather generally good; the valleys live under the shelter of the characteristic Chilcotin summer. There are wildflowers to suit your fancy, rushing streams, an emerald lake, and lots of timberline country.

GETTING THERE: From the southern end of Lillooet, cross the bridge over Seton Creek and approach the Shantyman Restaurant–Shell station. Turn left just west of the station and start along the West Road (which may be followed to the Lytton ferry). From the West Road turn-off, go 17.0 km to a sharp turn, a forest road, and a bridge. This is Texas Creek (0 km).

DESCRIPTION: This typical forestry road winds up a narrow, rocky gorge beside Texas Creek. The road crosses the creek at 1.9 km, 2.6 km and 3.9 km. Several picnic and camping spots are available.

To follow Texas Creek to its headwaters, stay left at 7.0

km. (The faint track to the right is the way to Molybdenite Lake and will be described below.)

Cross a new bridge at 7.6 km and enter the meadows.

At 11.3 km a branch goes off to the left up Skimath Creek. It is a new logging road which goes only 2.0 km. Stay right on the main road.

Cross a cattle guard at 12.3 km. It was in this section of the road that we came across a very plump, very sleek black bear—who fortunately high-tailed it into the brush.

The fork at 15.4 km presents a dilemma. Both branches lead to equally attractive high country. The left (south) branch cuts across the meadows to 20.0 km, where it forks once again. Both forks end shortly afterwards. About half-way along the southern fork there is a wranglers' camp. The mountains at the head of this valley are perhaps more spectacular than those of the north fork, but probably not as accessible.

The right (north) fork may be followed to 18.5 km and a broken bridge. The small bridge remains in good condi-

Indian paintbrush at Texas Creek (Keith Thirkell photo)

tion; it has just slipped off one bank of the stream into the river. An industrious crew might be able to figure out a way to use it. In any case, the road turns uphill to the left and ends in a log patch. This is one approach to some of the mountains in the area.

Both branches of Texas Creek are easy driving, which should present no difficulty to either four-wheel drive cars or trucks.

Molybdenite Lake: Return to the fork at 7.0 km. This trail is easily missed. If you come to the fifth (new) bridge you will have to backtrack. The way to Molybdenite Lake requires some effort and is a Class 5 four-wheel drive.

After a short, steep section, the trail switchbacks a couple of times and then strikes out across the rockslides (8.6 km) that have been dumped from the cliffs above towards Molybdenite Creek below. At first they are merely annoying, but they become more challenging as you climb higher up the valley. The worst section is near the end, as the trail begins to enter thicker forest.

After the rocks, plunge through some brush as the road temporarily levels out. At 13.6 km pass a beautiful camp with several abandoned buildings. The most habitable of them had been recently swept when we were there, and the entire site was pleasantly free of garbage or scars.

At 14.1 km another faint track strikes off to the right up a subsidiary valley. This path eventually works its way up to timberline and then zigzags up a large bald mountain, nearly to the summit.

Stay left and you will reach Molybdenite Lake, but not before climbing along the mountain on the north side of the creek. The path is steep, cut by several small streams and a waterfall, and a bit "hippy" in some places.

The last section is the steepest, but the road drops down to a campsite at 18.0 km. There is a brook on one side, the lake in front, and a curtain of crenellated mountain faces behind. The space available for camping is small—no more than two or three trucks at the most.

The lake is as far as it is practical to drive. The trail switchbacks up and divides about .5 km farther on. The left branch is blocked by various boulders and eventually by a huge rockslide. One branch of this road drops down to a small pond in a high basin beneath the peak across Molybdenite Lake; the other goes within a two-hundred-foot scramble of the col. The branch that doubles back east is also blocked, and leads to mine diggings in a pass above.

From the camp it is possible to reach the high ridges with no difficulty. To the south, the low point in the ridge may be reached in thirty or forty minutes, even if you pause at one of the ponds along the way. From there, an easy hike will take you east to a long summit and an even longer view. The jagged summit in the foreground across the lake is not, as it appears, the highest in the area. That distinction is reserved for the gentle summit to the right.

TIFFIN CREEK/TIM COLE FOREST ROAD
Rating: 2

The Tiffin Creek/Tim Cole Forest Road climbs from the Fraser Canyon over Mount Cole and down to Marble Canyon Park on Highway 12, bypassing the historic site of Pavilion. The upper section of the road provides good views. (See map page 112.)

GETTING THERE: From the junction of the road out of Lillooet and Highway 12, turn north. Follow Highway 12 for 23 km to the turn-off (right) marked Tiffin Creek Forest Road. This road is just to the south of the second of two new bridges.

DESCRIPTION: The Tiffin Creek road winds uphill along the slopes of Mount Cole, around the headwaters of Kealley Creek, then curves back south (6 km) and joins the Tim Cole Forest Road.

Follow the Tim Cole road southeast, then north to a shoulder, where it begins zig-zagging down the mountain

Four-wheelers at Tiffin Creek, on the Tim Cole Forest Road

in a series of sharp curves. The road exits onto Highway 12 at the east end of Tourquoise Lake in Marble Canyon Park.

 ## YALAKOM ROAD
Rating: 4

The Yalakom Road climbs from a dry shelf near Moha to an abandoned high-altitude mining camp on Poisonmount Creek. Along the way there are several bypaths worth exploring, some delightful meadows, and plenty of places to dip your toes in the stream. The Yalakom is quite popular with backroaders, but there are a variety of campsites along the way. Overall, the trail presents few difficulties, the greatest danger being a cut tire from sharp rocks. However, the upper reaches of the road may be clogged by snow well into mid-summer.

This is a fairly lengthy trip and it is a good idea to thoroughly check your provision list and fill your gas tank

The upper Yalakom Valley

before leaving Lillooet. I recall coming across one hungry couple, newcomers to BC, who got far up the valley to a secluded campsite before they realized that this wasn't like southern Ontario, where it is normal to pitch camp and drive to the nearest village for food.

GETTING THERE: Drive north through Lillooet, turning left at the Mohawk station onto the road to Carpenter Lake. Pass the Slok Forest Road turn-off on the right, and continue for 31 km to the junction of the roads to Bralorne (left) and Moha (right). Stay right. The road is now level plateau far above the Bridge River, and at 32 km the Yalakom Road (sign) goes right (0 km).

DESCRIPTION: The road climbs gradually through dry forest. There are usually cattle on the road. At 8 km cross a bridge. Yalakom Road here becomes the Yalakom Forest Road and begins to climb more steeply.

At 10 km a road left indicates the way to Lake Lemare. Lake Lemare is a short short four-wheel drive ascent. Stay right at most forks. It is a tiny lake with a campsite barely big enough for a couple of trucks. The Yalakom route continues to the right.

At 10.4 km cross a bridge, stay right. At 14 km pass a side road on the left. The trail now follows the stream for a distance, crossing it at 15 km. At 16 km stay right. There is a small campsite near the bridge to the left.

The next 4 km are relatively steep, rising along the side of the mountain, then dropping back down towards the creek. There are nice views, but it is probably better to pay attention to the road, which is relatively narrow.

At 21.7 km there is another campsite on the valley floor. The trail climbs again and then drops back into the valley. A side road (right) at 26 km leads to a secluded campsite. The road becomes a shelf road with a gorge on the left.

Cross the creek and go right at 30 km, winding uphill past a strange pyramidal rock formation on the right, then dropping back again and crossing a bridge at 32 km.

At 34.5 km ford a small stream, and pass a hunter's camp at 36.2. At 38 km a side road enters from the left. This is probably the old Blue Creek Road, once part of a pack trail. Some years ago we followed it up to a narrow little ridge, but were stopped by snow.

At 38.9 pass a cabin and enter an old burn area. Cross the bridge at 41.8 and head up the slope again. The road is becoming quite a bit rougher, and the sidehills more challenging.

Be careful at 43 km. There is a tricky, sharp left turn. Drivers may have their attention diverted by the cabin to the right.

The trees are getting smaller as the road gains altitude. At 44.6 pass another side road on the left and then enter a gentle area with several wet meadows. Cross the creek at 48.5 km, pass another cabin at 49 km and arrive at the old

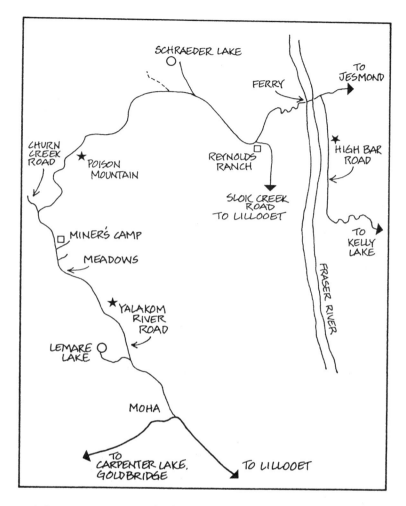

mining camp at 51 km. The mining camp consists of a couple of old shacks and several stacks of core samples neatly arranged in long boxes. Several short tracks lead out to old drill holes. We found core samples with definite streaks of gold: fool's gold, I presume.

The road forks here, with the left fork heading to higher country, more meadows, and eventually the Mud Lakes/China Head junction.

POISON MOUNTAIN—CHINA HEAD
Rating: 6

On a clear day you can see forever. Or so it seems from the windswept summit of China Head. This tiny trail ascends to the head of the Yalakom Valley and the treeline, then turns east and follows the broad summits, before dropping down to the road system leading to Slok Forest Road and Big Bar ferry.

The rewards offered by this trip are very great indeed, but several cautionary notes are in order. This is a long trip requiring plenty of food, equipment, and fuel. The closest gas station at the *end* of the trail is 65 km away. Your truck should be in good condition. Secondly, this is a challenging route. One can expect to encounter snowdrifts, swollen streams and deep crossings, treacherous sidehills, and a lot of downed timber blocking the path. Many of the hazards are on the far end of the trip, and therefore make it harder to retreat.

Third, the trail crosses very fragile alpine meadows. This is no place to prove to your companions how great your vehicle is at doing damage to the earth. Follow the beaten path with no deviations, hike to the viewpoints, and remember that the carelessness of a few can lead to prohibitions against everyone. Finally, this is a trip for July or August; snow usually renders it impassable until far into the summer.

GETTING THERE: From Lillooet take the Carpenter Lake Road to Yalakom Road, follow the Yalakom for 51 km to the old mining camp.

DESCRIPTION: Cross the stream (0 km) and take the left (straight) trail uphill. Pass an old line cabin on your left at 1.3 km, then cross the stream and start up the right side of the valley. At 2.1 km the trail crosses the stream again.

The fork in the road in the middle of a broad meadow at

3.5 km indicates that the Mud Lakes Forest Road is to the left, the China Head Road is to the right. Stay right.

The trees are now thinning out as you approach timberline. Stay right at various sidepaths and arrive at the first broad viewpoint at 4.7 km. Enter into a patch of small trees and drop down steeply, crossing a stream at 6.4 km. There are some sidehills on this section.

Another stream is crossed at 7.8 km. The side road back to the Yalakom is on the right at 8.3 km. The road to the left and China Head now makes five or six stream crossings. Several of these are relatively deep. The drier sections have some sidehills caused by erosion of the slope. Pass a small campsite at 10.1 km.

The track is getting rougher as it ascends to timberline once again at 14.2 km. The mountain to the left is appropriately named "Red Mountain." Should you have the good fortune to be travelling on a clear sunny day the view from the bump at 15.4 km will be much appreciated.

The trail next drops into scrub forest heading along the

Timberline on the Poison Mountain trail

The end of the Poison Mountain–China Head trail

Looking east towards Upper Big Bar Road

ridge. Pass a side road on the right, and another at 20.1. This is a summit road for another view.

As the trail descends into thicker and thicker forest, it becomes narrow, twisting and often blocked by downed trees. At 24.1 km there is a track to the left, leading to a miner's shack and a clearcut area.

At 25.1 km pass a tiny, one-truck campsite which is perched on a rock overlooking the valley.

Loggers are rapidly obliterating the old road, working up the ridge building a modern logging superhighway. I came across skidders and a crew at 28 km. The China Head trail meets the mainline logging road at 29.3 km.

From this junction with the mainline logging road, the traveller may go left past the new Pony Valley logging road, to the sidetrail leading into a Forest Service campsite at Schraeder Lake (4.5 km), or right towards Big Bar. I understand that the mainline logging road continues past the Schraeder Lake turn-off and eventually ends at a bluff overlooking the Fraser River. If you choose to go right, the turn-off to the Slok Forest Road (which leads to Lillooet) is 9 km, and the Big Bar ferry across the Fraser is 18 km.

On the way out to Slok Road or Big Bar, you will pass the South French Bar Creek turn-off (on the right) at 1.7 km. Cross the bridge and take the upper road to the right. This becomes a shelf road above a lake (with a road to the lake at the far end), and then at 9 km divides at the Big Bar/Slok Road junction. The Slok Forest Road has been much improved in the past five years. It is no longer a series of mud-puddles.

The Big Bar Road continues towards the river. At 13 km pass the Reynolds Ranch gate and a sign stating that the ferry is 7 km, Jesmond 27, and Route 97 is 97 km. Meaning: you are still a long way from the nearest paved highway or service station.

Once past the Reynolds Ranch, the road switchbacks precipitously down the mountainside in dry country to the muddy banks of the Fraser. Save some film for the views, but drivers should keep their eyes on the road, since a small mistake could lead to a big tumble. The ferry runs in summertime and is free. On the far side the road heads towards Jesmond, and from Jesmond either east to Highway 97, or south along the Jesmond Road to Kelly Lake.

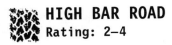

HIGH BAR ROAD
Rating: 2–4

This road is like a light dessert after a full meal on China Head. The High Bar is essentially a tortuous ranch road, running through the Reserve and servicing several ranches on the shelf above the Fraser River. The main attractions are the views of the Fraser River as it winds its way through gorges, high bluffs and dry country like a miniature Grand Canyon. The relatively high rating given to this route derives from the last section of the road which is very steep and very narrow, with lots of hairpin curves. I was grateful that I met no one coming in the other direction and that it was a perfectly dry day. On a wet day this may be a trip for High Anxiety.

As the signage informs you, much of this road is on aboriginal land and *all* hunting or fishing is prohibited.

GETTING THERE: From Jesmond drive west to the hill just above the reaction ferry (19 km). From the Big Bar Ferry drive up the hill and turn right at the signs (0 km).

DESCRIPTION: The road immediately becomes a narrow little path which turns in and out of the gullies, passing irrigated fields on the more level sections. Pass a farm at 9.8 km.

At 14.8 a fork right is signed "High Bar Ferry Road." This does not lead to an active ferry, but a river crossing used by ranchers on the west bank with their own boats. Stay left and uphill.

Stop at 16.5 km and enjoy the view. To the right of the large gully on the far side is the Ward Ranch, to the left the old Dunroven cart track, and the buildings of the old High

Bar ferry. At 20 km pass a ranch and gear down for a steep downhill section.

At 25 km pass the gate of Bavarian Ranch and start uphill. I wisely locked my hubs here. The sign says the next section is a mere 23% grade. But it doesn't tell you that the corners on the switchbacks are tight, the road narrow, the grade unrelenting. If your rig heats up, carry water.

It was with some relief that I reached the end of the steep section at 29 km. The road now travels through relatively thick forest with a few cabins and joins the Jesmond Road at 34 km. Turn right to get to Kelly Lake. It was another 9.4 km to Kelly Lake and the Pavilion road. (*Note:* if you need gas, Clinton (16 km to the left) is closer than Lillooet.)

Heading for the hills

Debating the meaning of the map

Section 10
OUTFITTING FOR FOUR-WHEELING

It all started with the Jeep. Thousands of Allied soldiers got their first taste of four-wheeling in one of the little four-cylinder military vehicles built by a variety of manufacturers under license between 1941 and 1950. My father bought a used Jeep (built by Ford) in 1949. I remember its emergency hand-operated windshield wipers and fuel pump, harshly grinding gear shift, tiny hard kapok seats, and nifty little compartments over the wheel wells. Although the Jeep's top speed was about 50 kph, it would go anywhere: through mud, high water, up abandoned wagon tracks to old ghost towns and obscure lakes. I loved it.

Today virtually all car and truck manufacturers produce some kind of four-wheel drive vehicle. It is ostensibly a consumer's paradise, but it is not easy to choose a vehicle because they are marketed like beer and cosmetics. Separating the quality of the suspension system from the sunset in a television commercial is no easy task. In such a market, the prospective buyer can only make a list of many wishes, priorize them and seek to find the vehicle that comes closest to the ideal. All I can do here is offer a few hints.

CHOOSING A PROPER VEHICLE: 4WD CARS VS 4WD TRUCKS

I use the term "truck" to include the standard pickups, the so-called "utility vehicles" which are frequently a four-wheel drive station wagon on a truck chassis, and the "jeeps" which include the smaller, sportier YJ, Suzuki and Tracker vehicles. The range in size, style, and especially price is enormous, but the expectation that the vehicle will be better on snow, up a rough rocky trail, or through a patch to mud is the same whether it is a $14,000 Jeep or a $60,000 Range Rover.

Whatever the price, all true off-road vehicles have some common characteristics. First, the frame, body, suspension and undercarriage of these trucks are built to avoid the abuse of rough terrain, and absorb any abuse that cannot be avoided. Differentials are encased in heavier metal; transfer cases are tucked underneath and protected by skid plates. Heavy duty springs and shocks are standard. Wheel wells may be larger to accommodate the installation of larger tires. Ground clearance is higher.

Second, the drive trains of four-wheel drive trucks are different from your average highway chariot. Power is distributed to all four wheels, not just two. This means that the wheels are both pulling and pushing at the same time. It means more control on washboard roads, the ability to climb over uneven terrain. The power from the engine is put into the low rpm range, giving the driver an easier start when pulling a heavy load and, equally important, maximum torque when crawling up a steep hill. Off-road trucks are haulers, not sprinters, work horses not race horses.

Third, the gearing of off-road vehicles has a higher ratio in both low and high range. The drive shaft turns three-and-a-half to five times for every revolution of the wheel in low range. This enables you to crawl over rocks slowly, using the engine's power at full throttle for relentless

Meadow running

traction without spinning the wheels. The combination of high torque and low gearing gives the four-wheel drive vehicle an advantage over two-wheel drive and four-wheel drive cars. This combination also permits the installation of larger-than-stock tires without too much loss of power.

Some trucks come with lockers or limited slip differentials, a gearing system that transfers the power to the wheels touching the ground. A standard differential will transfer power to the wheel which is spinning fastest, i.e. the outside wheel on a curve or the one which is spinning uselessly in the air. Limited slip transfers the power to the tires on the ground, enabling the four-wheeler to creep up an uneven slope without spinning. This is a disadvantage on the highway, but a great advantage off-road. (After-market versions of limited slip allow the driver to choose whether or not to use this system.)

Finally, a large variety of modifications are possible for the standard four-wheel drive vehicles. This "after-market" equipment allows owners to improve performance and customize the machine to meet specific wants and needs.

A basic decision is the type of truck to buy. The popularity of pickup trucks is more than a matter of price. It has the appearance of practicality; you can always promise to do chores like hauling leaf rakings to the dump. On the other hand, everyone wants you to help them move into their new suite. Pickup beds hold a lot of gear, and if you bolt on a canopy it is easy to roll out a foam pad and sleep in the back. The disadvantages include the lack of space for riders. Aunt Zelda may not appreciate having to ride in the back with the tool kit, jerry cans and high lift jack. The jump seats on most of the extra cab trucks are suitable only for smaller children.

Utility vehicles have all the comforts of a station wagon. However, you are paying a premium for convenience, style and comfort. They carry more passengers, are easier to pack and unpack, and are good town vehicles. However, they usually don't have the gear ratios, ground clearance, or suspension system of a regular truck.

The romance of four-wheeling has spawned the Jeep YJ, Suzuki, Trackers, etc. On the upside, they are sporty, spritely, and maneuverable in tight situations. They tend to be less costly than pickup trucks and sport utility vehicles. On the downside, they are often not as rugged as true off-road vehicles, they compensate for small engines with very low gear ratios, and you can't sleep in them. Sometimes they are a little narrow for the ruts in our BC logging roads. Yet they can be fun to drive, and I have seen a few that were intelligently modified to be very serviceable off-road prowlers.

When it comes to trucks, bigger is not necessarily better. Sure, a full-size pickup with an eight-cylinder engine is great for chewing your way through a deep mudhole, and its sheer weight will hold the vehicle to the ground on a rugged slope. And if you're the kind of person who eats the weight of an engine block for breakfast, a full-size truck will haul a week's grub for you. But you can also find it difficult to squeeze between boulders or make sharp switchback turns. Big trucks eat gas; that means carrying several dangerous and noxious jerry cans of extra fuel. And when one of these brutes sinks into deep snow, they are helpless and hell to dig out.

Buying any motor vehicle involves a combination of technical knowledge and negotiating ability. Before you go window shopping, it is probably worth checking out back issues of the various four-wheel drive magazines, particularly because they provide useful technical data about horsepower, torque and gear ratios. However be wary of the reported "tests" and competitions; they are typically beauty pageants administered by journalists who live in Los Angeles.

In rating a particular model, look for the following: road clearance, angle of departure (i.e. will the rear end drag crossing a ditch), turning radius, large size gas tanks, limited slip differentials, not too much stuff below the axles on the undercarriage, wheel wells large enough to take bigger tires and a good warranty. A basic model may be a better bet than one with an "off-road package," if the latter means power windows, air conditioning and other sissy stuff.

Next, you might talk to experienced four-wheelers about their vehicles. The four-wheel community is full of partisans—the Ford versus Chevy controversy goes back to my grandfather's time. The main question you want to ask is how often their truck has broken down, and what kind of repair costs they have incurred.

Buying a used 4 X 4 can be risky and exhausting, a road full of potholes. Buy from a friend and you risk losing the friend when the drive shaft breaks the first weekend. Car lots are full of near wrecks passed from one car auction to another without ever being sold. New car dealers want to sell new trucks, not trade-ins. And private ads may send you on a wild goose chase to check out a "mint condition" machine with crankcase oil the colour of hot chocolate and a frame that crooks to the left.

But the popularity of four-wheel drive vehicles dictates that there are some "good deals." Maybe they are Forerunners with running boards, the Ranger with desert running lights (i.e. never driven through a low hanging BC forest) or the carefully maintained pride and joy of a moderate four-wheeler. Which is the best buy? The truck that was never driven off-road, or the truck that was well looked after by an aficionado?

STOCK VS AFTER-MARKET

There must be a happy medium between a bone stock vehicle off the dealer's lot and an obsessively improved rig that looks like a Victorian drawing room. Most serious four-wheelers will make some changes and additions, but there is no need to go overboard. The four-wheel drive magazines are very much like the so-called "women's magazines," which both fuel and feed on anxiety. "Do you have sex appeal?" "Is your diff strong enough?" "Five ways to test your complexion." "Ten tests for axle sag." The magazines would have you spend $30,000 on the perfect truck, and then spend another $75,000 replacing every part. The

Negotiating a drainage ditch

articles and advertisements push the owner to replace everything from door locks to differential gearing.

On the other hand, the optimist who buys a truck and drives it ruthlessly, relying only on his warranty, is very likely to find himself up a creek, waving his warranty at a stuck truck and hoping for the arrival of a dealer's representative. Some changes and additions are reasonable:

TIRES: The larger, tougher meat eaters we see on 4 X 4 trucks are not all vanity. Larger diameter tires add crucial ground clearance; wider tracks improve traction; knobbier treads and thick sidewalls provide better grip under certain conditions. The preference among British Columbia four-wheelers is clearly for mud-terrain tires. Not only do they chew up mud, they are also good on loose rock. Thick sidewalls provide an extra area of potential traction on the loose stuff. In snow, however, mud-terrains are mediocre— you can't have everything. The soft treads won't wear as well as street tires, and they produce a constant highway hum which is music to some, an annoyance to others.

How big? Generally, serious four-wheelers limit themselves to something in the 31-inch, 10-50 range. Overly large tires may mean new wheels (expensive), less room for wheel travel, and a reduction of the gearing ratios (every gear seems like overdrive). Very large tires mean very large (and expensive) modifications. Monster tires usually indicate a street vehicle, not an off-road explorer.

SUSPENSION LIFTS: Some attempt to lift the truck accompanies the installation of larger tires. The goal is to provide more space for those big tires in the wheel wells, to increase the clearance under the transfer case, and to provide better handling on rough terrain through a stiffer ride—a worthy and practical goal. On some trucks a "modest" lift (note how the language is that of fashion and vanity) is relatively easy: an extra leaf spring on each rear axle, new coils in the front and new shock absorbers, adding a couple of inches all around.

With independent front suspension—and most trucks have this now—it is not nearly so easy. More complicated stock suspension systems and more "immodest" lifts require extensive modifications. An immodest lift can create serious problems for every component of the front suspension and steering system: pitman arms at the wrong angle, panhard rods that are too short, reduced turning ability. The sharper angles created by a lift will place more stress on U-joints, sometimes open the seals to the transfer case, etc., etc.

A specially designed kit available from one of the many US suppliers of these things is probably better than any attempt at home automotive engineering, but even here the buyer should be warned that it doesn't always fit, doesn't always work as well as the magazines say.

SHOCK ABSORBERS: Larger tires and changes to the suspension system usually must be accompanied by new shock absorbers. The ones that come with the truck are usually too soft and not suited to backroad conditions. Quick response gas shocks are popular because they are designed to keep the wheels on the ground no matter how uneven it is (with a consequent stiffness or roughness, which street drivers do not like).

WINCHES: Winches are:
- dangerous. Improper use can literally risk your neck;
- delicate. Even some of the major brands have a tendency to leak oil, and probably only about half of the winches gracing the front ends of four-wheel drive trucks actually work;
- hard on batteries. Most serious four-wheelers will cram a second battery under the hood somewhere;
- not a cure-all. Yes, Virginia, there are places where a winch won't help: if you have drowned out your engine in the middle of a stream, or are too far from any place to attach the cable, to name a couple;
- expensive;

- easily stolen;
- best used by someone who knows how to use one;
- a godsend in certain situations.

The folklore of four-wheeling is replete with tales of snapped cables that blasted out windshields, or scythed the brush for thirty feet. Local scientists have been puzzled for years over reports of a Sasquatch roaming the Harrison Lake area in a tattered jacket with a blue and green emblem. Now the true story can be told. In the early days, before the Lionsgaters Four Wheel Drive Club learned how to drive, they used to get stuck a lot. One day a fellow got in over his hubs up Harrison Lake. His companion hooked up the winch and draped a club jacket over the cable to reduce the snapback of the cable should it break. It did break, flinging the jacket into the bush, where it just happened to land on a curious Sasquatch who had come to see what was going on.

Tiptoeing across a rock slide

CB RADIO: Gone are the days when the airwaves were full of citizen band chatter; that fad seems to have been replaced by skateboards. CB radios may still be purchased, and they are a valuable addition to a four-wheeler's truck. Radio contact between comrades increases the fun and safety of any adventure, and a radio provides a modest margin of safety (CB radios don't work very well if you are stuck in a mountain gorge, or are a hundred kilometres from the nearest indoor plumbing) should you need to use Channel 9.

Cellular phones are handy, but no substitute for a CB radio. CB radios are for communicating within a group, the cellular phone is for calling home to say that you will be a little late. That is, if you aren't too far from the electronic highway to make a connection.

OTHER WORTHY ITEMS: Lots of additional gimmicks and improvements are just waiting at the supplier to be purchased. The ones listed above are crucial, but brush guards, fog lights, skid plates, nerf bars, etc., all have some practical advantages. Let your pocketbook decide.

A NOTE ABOUT EQUIPMENT: Late one autumn afternoon a couple of years ago, a friend and I offered to go out searching for some lost horses in the Gunn Creek area. Jon had a brand-new pickup truck and was eager to go four-wheeling for a good cause. We roared around some snowy logging roads, finding no evidence of the horses but lots of rough terrain. Just at dusk, Jon wanted to climb an attractive little hill, but it was too steep and too slick for his street tires. The truck started to slip, the front end took a nose dive off the side of the road, and the front wheels became lodged between two parallel logs. We were stuck.

We had only a small jack, no shovel, no chains, no come-along, no winch, no working CB radio and only light clothes (except for me—I had a down jacket). We tried for several hours to free the truck, working up quite a lather in the increasingly cold night air. Finally we gave up for the night and sat in the cab till morning, when we managed to lift the front end up by jacking up one axle and pushing in some logs, then jacking up the other side and doing the same thing until we could back off.

Meanwhile, our friends were scouring the countryside looking for us. We missed a fine dinner and scared our loved ones. We were lucky. The moral of this true life adventure is simple: do not go into the backcountry without the proper equipment.

A PERSONAL TRIP LIST

Everyone has their own personal needs and preferences. Rather than attempting to provide a perfect list, I offer my own list to give the reader something to chew on. I do try to check off things from my list as I load them into the truck. Usually I forget something anyway.

Clothes

two pairs of running shoes (one or both always get wet)
light hiking boots (in case we have to walk home)
spare socks
extra blue jeans
hiking shorts (for Lytton when the temperature is 41 C)
flannel or wool shirt
sweater
down jacket (for Lytton when it is 0 C)
wool hat
gloves
rain parka
old coat (to wear by the campfire when sparks are flying)

Personal

Swiss army knife
sunglasses
keys

money, credit card
belt pack to hold the above items
pen and notebook
battery-powered shaver
toothbrush/toothpaste
towel
soap and shampoo
toilet paper
mosquito repellent
sunburn cream
flashlight and extra batteries
first aid kit

Technology

camera, film, lens brush, tripod
binoculars
compass
maps
guidebooks
auto manual
chainsaw and fuel
Swede saw
shovel
hi-lift jack
tug strap
chain
tool box
air pump
jerry can with gas
two litres of engine oil
hammer

Camping equipment

sleeping bag
foam pads
tent and pegs
tarp (to cover tailgate while cooking in rain)
Coleman stove

propane
box with silverware, spatulas, tongs, etc.
bowls/paper plates, cups, wine glass
nesting pots
frying pan
thermos
ice chest/ice
dishrag/soap/paper towel
matches
coffee and paper filters
salt/pepper/spices

Luxuries

folding chair
small folding table
book

I manage to pack most of these items into some large plastic panniers. Ideally, one travels with enough to maintain comfort, but not so much as to make loading and unloading a chore. The comforts closest to the skin are obviously the most important. Propane-powered refrigerators seem to be more weight than worth it on most trips, but I have been uncomfortable because I did not have a pair of tweezers or fingernail clippers.

Section 11
LEARNING TO DRIVE AND DRIVING TIPS

Even the most mud hungry, rock crunching 4 X 4 does not drive itself. It takes skill and experience to get the most out of an expensive rig. Off-road driving cannot be learned overnight, nor from a book, but must be mastered through practice. Beginning rock climbers do not start out on the biggest walls; beginning skiers do not leap off cornices on their first outing. The same is true for four-wheelers: start easy and work up to the hard stuff.

Good teachers can help a beginner learn more quickly. A four-wheelers' club is an ideal place to meet more experienced drivers who will be glad to show you the ropes. Riding shotgun with a good driver a few times can be instructive. Watching others make mistakes, even listening to four-wheeling chatter over the CB radio, increases your understanding without wiping out your truck.

In time you will begin to get a feel for your truck, to know the limits and capabilities of the vehicle. Along with this will come greater confidence and better judgment. The true expert in any sport makes advanced skills look very simple. An ungainly Jeep driven by a good driver looks almost graceful as it dances up a rockpile. And since one of the penalties of inexperience is damage to the rig, the more skill at hand, the less expense to the owner.

GETTING TO KNOW YOUR VEHICLE

A surprisingly large number of four-wheelers who are willing to tackle a boulder-strewn backcountry trail, cannot tell you whether their differential housing is on the right, left or centre of the axle, or how many inches of clearance they have at the lowest point of the undercarriage. Before you lock the hubs, spend a few minutes underneath the truck learning where the low points are, familiarizing yourself with anything—handbrake cables, steering arms, etc.—that might snag on an errant branch or sharp rock.

Learn the width of a vehicle and how the tires track—especially when turning sharp corners. Do not forget the height of the vehicle either, and remove any apparatus (desert running lights, carrying racks) that might catch on low-hanging branches. Do you know the angles of approach and departure of the truck? When will the front bumper gouge dirt going through a dip? When will your rear end drag?

Basic physics translated into mathematical formuli can be used to determine when any object will tip over. Auto and sailboat suppliers sell simple gauges to determine the degree of tilt and thus warn you of the inadvertent application of nature's laws. Both formuli and gauges should be used with caution. They are basic physics all right, but laboratory physics under controlled conditions. The loading of a full ice chest on the driver's side, or the presence of a small rock on a tilting slope, may alter the truck's centre of gravity. Knowing when the tilt is too much may be as much a second sense as a scientific analysis.

Every make and model of truck handles a bit differently in the woods. Tables and charts showing maximum horsepower and torque must be applied to actual driving condi-

Halting a slide down hill

tions. Some trucks (typically an unloaded pickup) are light in the back end, others heavy. Some vehicles have short lock-to-lock steering wheels, others much longer. Large tires will limit the lock-to-lock movement. The visibility over the hood of a full-size Blazer is a lot less (especially if you are short) than through the windshield of a Suzuki. Nothing is more idiosyncratic, more a matter of individual touch, than the clutch. Suspension systems may be hard and stiff or soft and loose, making a big difference on a bumpy road. Some trucks with conventional carburetors will tend to stall going uphill, others going downhill. Knowing which description fits your truck can be a useful bit of information.

As mentioned above, owners of 4 X 4s should have a regular maintenance plan and should inspect their vehicles both before and after a trip. Such chores save grief in the long run. Almost every driver (the author included) has started charging up a hill in low range, noticed something funny, and then realized that the hubs were not locked. Tape a message to yourself on the dashboard until you learn to remember. Don't forget to check the hubs before going back on the highway—in fact, check them twice.

DRIVING

First-rate off-road driving skill combines strategy, tactics and finesse. Or, in other words, standout route finding, driving techniques and seat-of-the-pants responsiveness. Add only the ingredient of common sense and you have an expert driver.

STRATEGY: Like tennis players, but unlike golfers, we play in confined spaces. The sidelines of our sport are rivers, cliffs, fallen trees, ruts, rocks and mud. Like a battlefield general, a good driver chooses an objective and finds the best way to advance towards it with the least cost.

Route-finding involves connecting short stretches of driving into a continuous line of attack, moving from one position to the next without getting hung up.

The four-wheeler as strategist peers through the mist, assessing such factors as:
- obstacles on, beside and above the trail;
- steepness and the amount of power necessary to get up;
- character of the ground: patches of soft dirt, loose rock, hard rock, mud;
- angle of the side slope and anything (like a rock or ledge) that would affect tilt;
- narrow spots, especially curving ones that can hang up a bumper or cause the rear end of a long wheelbase rig to fall off;
- any danger points like weak cribbing, rotten bridgework, soft shoulders;
- difficulties of retreat, including assessing which way the truck will slide if it loses traction;
- possible winch points.

All these factors are combined in some mysterious mental calculation that produces a plan of attack. The driver hopes to know exactly where all four wheels will be at any given moment. It only takes one wheel off the road to snatch defeat from the jaws of victory. In short, a good driver thinks first and drives second. Usually this can be done during continuous driving, but sometimes it is necessary to get out of the cab and walk the route. This is where friends help: they can push rocks around, suggest alternatives to the original plan of attack, and help guide you over the tough spots.

TACTICS: The elements of strategy are tactics, the individual maneuvers used to reach an objective. Although every trail is unique, the four-wheeler will confront certain problems time and time again. It follows that a standard bag of tricks or tactics is the normal stuff of off-roading.

Hill Climbing

Loss of traction means loss of forward motion and often loss of control. Therefore, inspect the terrain carefully to identify soft spots and hard spots (like ledges that will bounce a wheel in the air or shove the wheel into the wheel well beyond the truck's range of axle travel).

Carefully choose the gear you will use, and stick with it. A hill should be approached with a good head of steam— not recklessly, but with enough power to carry you over the top, not so much that the wheels begin to spin.

When the going gets tough and you start to lose traction, "walk" the wheels up; swing the steering wheel from side to side and increase the amount of traction on the sidewalls.

If one wheel hits a ledge and won't go over, another wheel spins uselessly in the dirt and you start to stall, don't try to take the rig over by slipping the clutch. You may, however, be able to get a rocking motion started: let the truck slip backwards a few inches and then go forward. This rocking motion is a good trick to learn.

If the engine stalls on a steep slope, it isn't always necessary to depress the clutch. Just turn the key with the clutch engaged.

Downhill

Descents in mountain climbing are always more dangerous than ascents. I suspect the same is true in four-wheeling. Certainly nothing freezes the tailbone to the seat
quicker than a loss of control coming down a steep, winding
shelf road. Gravity seems to aid and abet the enemy.

Keep off the brakes. Gear down before you go rocketing
off the top of the slope, and let the engine work with you
while all four wheels are turning. Brake-locked wheels are
dead wheels.

If you start to lose control and are not cramped for space,
press down on the accelerator. As in skiing, a moderate
amount of speed increases control.

Avoid turning your wheels sharply. A cramped wheel
will often start to skid in the opposite direction. You want
to go left, the front end starts sliding to the right. Gentle,
gentle on the wheel.

Pay attention to drop-offs—and know your angle of
departure.

Sidehills and Slopes

British Columbia's weather is hard on trails. Bridges and
fords are the first to go. Then the banks and shoulders begin
to fill in and fall off, leaving the off-roader with some
potentially dangerous sidehill slopes to cross. I have
watched my front wheel hit and collapse an outside shoulder on a road with a five-hundred-foot fall. The only thing
to do was boot it and hope that the rear wheel would be
carried over the gap by the pull of the front wheels. Sidehills
can also be very touchy affairs; it is like playing Russian
roulette with gravity.

Don't guess. Dig. If you have any doubt about the angle
of the slope, stop and get out the shovels. Carve a rut for
the inside, uphill wheel to follow, making sure to dig out
room for your bumper on a steep slope. Use this rut as a
guide for your inside wheels. Try like the devil to ensure
that your rear wheel follows the same groove—otherwise
you may be in for trouble.

In climbing over a sidehill washout, aim your vehicle to make a smooth curve so that the rear end does not start sliding out from beneath you. This means aiming above the apex of the slope so that when your front wheels turn, the rear wheels follow the same track.

Should you start to slip, it may be best simply to press on the accelerator and hope that your momentum will carry you beyond the sidehill before you slip downhill.

Always watch the outside shoulder and avoid anything that looks like it will collapse. Again, it is better to spend one hour digging than four or five days recovering the pieces of your truck from the bottom.

Good Old Mud

Mud terrifies some, is pure pleasure for others. Mud gets your truck dirty and makes you look like a hero. Mud may be soft and watery, thick and sticky. Freudians have a lot of opinions about those who like mud.

Think about the rocks and logs and slimy dead frogs

Gumbo mud

lurking underneath the mud before you charge. Think also about what you are going to do if the mud hole is six feet deep, not one foot deep. Think about it anyway.

Don't tiptoe up to a muddy patch, charge it. And once you get going, do not stop. The resistance of mud on the tires is terrific; use enough power to carry you all the way through.

If you bog down, do not spin your wheels frantically. The poor truck will just sink deeper and deeper—meaning that you will have to dig deeper and haul more logs and bark to get yourself out.

If you find mud on the inside of your windshield it is probably because you left your window open and the rear tires were cleaning themselves properly.

What is true of mud is pretty much true of **sand**, although it is even easier to lose traction and sink into sand.

Rocks

Climbing rocks requires patience. The idea is not to blast through them, but to crawl over them.

Rock crawling

Water sports

Pay close attention to the kind of rock, watching out for the very sharp kind (shale) that will slice a sidewall like a knife slices butter.

Let the air out of your tires. Reduce the air pressure to 20 lbs. or so to increase your traction—and soften the ride. (Remember to fill them back up before driving on the highway.)

Pick a low gear and go slowly, letting the front wheel climb over and down the boulders.

Put your tires on a big rock rather than putting the rock through your oil pan. This is where long axle travel is nice.

Keep your foot off the clutch.

Don't be shy about asking a helper to move a rock that bothers you—get out and help him if it is a gutbuster.

Walk your wheels and use your sidewalls for additional traction, especially on loose, crumbly rock slopes.

When you scrape or hit something, do remember to get out and check for damage as soon as possible.

Digging through a snowbank

Water

Fording ankle-deep brooks is fun; fording knee-deep streams takes concentration; crossing anything deeper is downright dangerous. Club scrapbooks thrive on snapshots of Huey's truck floating downstream and Erma taking a bath in her cab. Deep water is risky and often extremely expensive.

Be prepared. Airscoops should be detached so that they don't suck water into the air filters and carburetor. The rubber tubing that vents the differentials should be extended. You may even consider detaching the fan belt, taping or slipping an old inner tube over the distributor, and running a rubber hose up from the exhaust. Also think about duct taping the doors—especially if your fuse box is almost on the floorboards.

Test the depth and current of the water. Wade across if necessary. Pay attention to any large boulders (sometimes visible by the river current) or sandspits on the river bottom. Avoid these.

Travel in a group equipped with winches and/or tow

straps. Hook the tow strap on your front end before you start across. Consider winching the truck across rather than driving it.

Attack the stream with enough power to get you across, remembering that stream beds are often irregular. Don't go so fast that you will increase the resistance of the water or splash water on your distributor. Once you start, keep going. The middle of a fast running stream is not the best place to pause for second thoughts.

Compensate for the current by heading upstream.

If your engine conks out, do not try to start it. Call for the winch.

Dry your brakes after the crossing.

Check your transmission, differentials, hubs, brakes, etc. for water contamination after you get home.

Snow

Snow is as various as rocks: wet snow, dry snow, deep snow, snow over ice, black ice, gritty ice, even chunks of ice. A few tips:

Don't try to plow into a snowbank at high speed; it may be more solid than you think.

Use narrow tires if you have them.

Learn how to control a skidding vehicle by reversing the normal turning of the wheels. Do not expect brakes to be much use in stopping—use your gears.

Use the highest gear possible, not the lowest.

Carry chains.

High Centring

In theory—a lot of good that does—no experienced driver should ever high centre his or her vehicle. Knowing how to avoid this embarrassment is part of learning the skills of four-wheeling. It happens to the best of them, but a slow, leisurely pace is one way to escape this fate.

Once you have high centred your vehicle there are four options:

- It is already too late—as the gouges on your transfer

case indicate—so just go ahead and be more careful next time.

- Back off and try again.
- Put rocks under the front wheels and back up onto them and over the hangup.
- Unlimber the old high-lift jack and push the truck sideways or forwards or backwards off the problem—or use a shovel to dismantle the obstacle.

Special Gremlins

British Columbia has some special gremlins. We have all heard about backroaders who cracked a differential on a particularly large and hard mound of grizzly scat. More commonly, however, our trails are full of old snags and logging slash that have a bad habit of jumping off the road and catching something underneath. The remedy for this is to watch out.

Equally inscrutable are those darn branches that want to pinstripe your paint job or smash your windshield. It is a good idea to roll up the rear windows so that stray branches do not end up mixing with your riders.

One does not have to be a geologist to note the difference between sharp rocks like shale and dull rocks like sandstone. The sharper the rocks on the road ahead, the more slowly and cautiously you should travel. It takes about three seconds for a pointy slab to empty a $200 tire of its air and its usefulness.

If you know anything about four-wheeling in British Columbia, you will know a lot about bears, mosquitos and blackflies. All three are perils of the backroader. BC has mosquitos so big that if you hit one head-on at 50 kph, its stinger will not only puncture your radiator but probably crack your engine block. Old timers suggest eating yeast or wearing light-coloured clothes, but there is nothing like a good coat of bear grease or a potent mosquito repellent. Blackflies seem to resist insect repellents. Wear thick clothing.

The bears of BC are big and dangerous. I knew a guy

who had to be winched out of a grizzly paw print in the Kootenays once. Even little bears can run faster than a human, and bigger ones are reported to attack pickup trucks in the Prince George area. Don't mess with bears. Don't leave a mess around for them to play with.

And finally, always wear your seat belt.

Section 12
ALONE OR WITH OTHERS

The image of 4 X 4s as "get away" vehicles is impressed upon us by advertisements that show solitary trucks and solitary men perched on hilltops, or speeding towards the setting sun on a spacious desert. Paradoxically, four-wheeling with others will expand the four-wheeler's opportunities and maximize the fun. The solution to the paradox is to do both.

The case for joining a four-wheel drive club (or forming one if necessary) is a strong one. Take into consideration the following:

Going with others (especially those with more experience) increases the margin of safety. Six or seven strong bodies can unstick a truck more easily and more quickly than one or two. The scope of mechanical skills (and probably the available parts and tools) is broader in a group.

Club members share notes and knowledge about places to travel. The trips described in this guidebook only scratch the surface of the possibilities, and new trails are being discovered every weekend by four-wheel drive clubs.

Then there is congeniality, and fun. It is more fun to share an adventure (even afterwards over beer), and many clubs have activities designed to incorporate non-four-wheeling family members.

Clubs are the places to learn about rallying, racing, mud runs, etc. There is more to four-wheeling than backcountry travel, and you might find some of these sports exciting.

Club members trade skills, parts, advice and assistance. Since keeping a machine in running order takes a lot of effort, you can benefit from any advantage.

Four-wheeling in our backcountry depends upon public understanding and tolerance. These come only because we have a voice, and our views are expressed through the province's four-wheel drive clubs. Road closures, restrictions and legislation on after-market equipment are the bane of our sport, and we need the clout of strong organizations behind us.

Four Wheel Drive Association rally

Clubs seek to serve the community as a way of expressing our sense of responsibility. We work with various charities and service organizations as good citizens.

I think the biggest reason many of the thousands of four-wheelers do not belong to a four-wheel drive club is simple human shyness. If you do not know anyone in a club, it is sometimes difficult to work up the courage to make contact with that club. When I got interested in four-wheeling, I wrote a letter to the Four Wheel Drive Association of BC (PO Box 284, Surrey, BC V3T 4W8), and promptly got a letter and a phone call in return. The club spokeswoman and I discussed the various clubs, and I was invited to come on a trip. She also gave me the name of the membership secretary of the club I eventually joined. Within a week, my wife and I had our brand-new truck out on an exciting trip. So don't be shy, join.

Not every BC community has a four-wheel drive club. If you would like advice on how to go about forming a club—and it is not that hard—contact the Four Wheel Drive Association of BC. Most of the clubs belong to the association, and we have links with similar organizations in the US. Members get the *Backroader*, which has reports of trips, articles on equipment, and information on club activities.

WOMEN AND FOUR-WHEELING

It would be less than honest to ignore the fact that off-roading is associated with machismo, or that some men who happen to own big trucks have not quite caught on to the changes in our society. Some women, on the other hand, think of Jeeps as deadly rivals who will steal their boyfriends away every weekend. This need not be true. If men recognize that women make great four-wheelers (after all, Michele Mouton was a Pike's Peak 4WD Hillclimb champion), and women are a little more assertive about demanding the right to take the wheel, then we will all have a lot more fun. Already, many of the stalwarts of our four-wheel drive clubs are women.

GOING SOLO

Sometimes we go alone out of choice, perhaps because we are just tired of crowds, perhaps because we want to savour the intensity that comes from being far from anywhere and anybody. I find myself paying a lot more attention to nature when I am camping alone or sitting in my truck watching the clouds swirl around a ridge. Solo four-wheeling makes me acutely conscious of what I am doing, and more careful about how I do it. When I get home, I am normal again.

There are several special rules for solo off-roading:
- Always tell someone where you are going and when you are coming back;
- Take extra tools, parts, food, clothing, flares, etc.;
- Check your vehicle out with extra care;
- Equip your rig with a working CB radio;
- Drive very carefully and cautiously.

Section 13
ETHICS OF FOUR-WHEELING

We share the outdoors with others, and we have a responsibility to protect it for our own use and for those who will follow us. Most of the four-wheel drive clubs stress the importance of good trail manners. What are good trail manners?

No littering. This means more than not flinging beer cans into the nearest lake. It means bringing back everything. Do not count on a campfire to incinerate cans, plastic, old socks, oil filters, etc. Always take along an empty trash bag, and always bring back a full one. If you are *really* responsible, you will collect a little and leave the trail cleaner than you found it.

Do not wreck trails. The plaudits and prizes for four-wheeling go to those who get up with the least damage, not the most.

No looting or vandalism. Leave cabins, mines and nature as you found them. Preventing vandalism is the strongest argument for closing trails, and we do not want trails closed.

Stay off meadows and pastures. Some environments are more delicate than others. Pastures and meadows are for gazing and grazing, not ripping up. Along with vandalism, this is the excuse others use to prevent us from enjoying the backcountry.

Fires. British Columbia has enough deadwood lying around that no camper should ever have to chop down a live tree. We have enough water that no campfire should ever be left in any state other than stone-cold dead. Watch the way the wind is blowing, and avoid peppering tinderbox under-growth with sparks. A small fire can warm and roast marshmallows as effectively as a huge bonfire. Pay atten-tion to fire regulations.

Respect others. Churning dust in the faces of hikers who are not so fortunate as to have a big truck like yours is no way to make friends or gain respect. It is far better to offer them a ride. Racing around narrow roads is not only dangerous, but is also a sure way to give the impression that four-wheelers are a bunch of nerds who should be caged.

Leave gates as you found them. If a gate is closed, it was probably meant to be closed; if it is open, it was left open on purpose.

Do not get in the way of others who are working. The guys driving logging trucks may be an annoyance to your holi-day, but they are just trying to make enough money to buy or maintain their own pickups.

Control the use of guns. Hunting deer is a sport. Blasting holes in stop signs, old cabins and old cars is vandalism for pea brains. If you really must shoot something worthless, try your foot.

Private property. The claims of those who own property are often exaggerated and unreasonable, but it is almost always better to ask permission than to bully the owner.

Section 14

OFF-ROADING AND HOW TO PROTECT IT

Four-wheelers in British Columbia are indeed fortunate. We have room to share the backcountry without getting in each other's way. Hikers and backpackers have enough trails to guarantee a lifetime of challenge without repetition. Climbers have enough trails and roads to timberline to eliminate the temptation to rent helicopters. And we have enough backcountry roads to whet the appetites of leisurely and tireless four-wheelers alike. Indeed, the only recreationist who has no place is the armchair conservationist who sits at home and dictates wilderness areas with the sweep of a hand.

The resource base of our economy will not, and should not, go away. If our forests are well managed (and debates over how to accomplish this are serious), we should have a continuing supply of primitive roads. Wise land use, public control, and public access should ensure that the logging roads of one decade become the four-wheel trails of the next, and the backpacker's bushwhack of the third.

The discussions leading to the recent Forest Practices Code more or less excluded recreational four-wheelers. Although Ministry studies indicate that recreational driving is among the most common post-harvest uses of forest lands, this fact seems to have played no role in the eventual outcome. Consequently, many backroads may be closed and even ploughed under. The loss to recreationists and to the public's right to watch over our forests may be devastating. Four-wheelers should report road closures, write to their MLAs about potential closures, and seek a fair hearing in implementation of the Forest Practices Code.

In order to obtain a fair hearing in the ongoing discussion of land use, we must be vigilant and must also show ourselves worthy of consideration by acting responsibly. Self-criticism is an essential part of the process, but so is clearing up some common misconceptions about four-wheeling.

A few people believe we go out into the woods to slaughter virgin wilderness. They do not understand that four-wheelers drive—or attempt to drive—over primitive roads, using an existing network of paths created by others. We are not trail blazers, and our explorations rarely retard the rapid natural decay of these backcountry tracks. Our interests spread us widely and thinly over a vast area, and we do not normally limit our fun to a few over-used areas. One reason for this guidebook is to encourage four-wheelers to sample more spots less often, reducing the impact of concentrated use. Land rapists we are not, but we do need to enlighten others to this fact.

We are often—but not always—unfairly blamed for all the trash and garbage left in the wilderness. The four-wheelers I know are conscious of this accusation, and seek to refute it by bringing back all their own trash and a little extra every trip.

There are, of course, individuals in every sport who are careless: cross-country skiers who think that trash buried in the snow will disappear by spring; slovenly hunters, fishermen, snowmobilers and mountain bikers. Black Tusk

Meadows and the Elfin Lakes Trail are not always pristine, and this cannot be blamed on four-wheelers. The club clean-up trip and the unpublicized personal policing of our campsites can set us apart from the others.

A third myth states that four-wheelers have imperialist designs on parks and protected recreational areas. It requires a highly inventive mind to believe that 4 X 4 owners want to cut roads through Garibaldi Park, since there is no evidence whatsoever of this desire. Four-wheelers, for the most part, prefer travel along unfrequented paths.

The antidote to these myths is greater public education of who we are and what we want. We don't want to be locked into a few designated paths or playgrounds any more than hikers want to be confined to sidewalks. We want to be able to share the outdoors, and our demands are both realistic and responsible.

We must also overcome some misconceptions we hold about ourselves. First and foremost, we cannot afford to resign ourselves to the idea that everyone is against us. It is tempting to romanticize ourselves into outlaws, and to come to the point where we are, in fact, our own worst enemies.

Second, we cannot go it alone. Although one of the dearest attractions of four-wheeling is the sense of self-reliance it engenders, we cannot afford to succumb to irresponsible anarchy. In modern societies, those who do not join with others are likely to get stepped on; it is no more onerous to attend a few club meetings every year than to hunt for hours for an unlocked gate.

Third, we should be seeking Canadian solutions to Canadian problems. In the US, the four-wheeling community often finds itself torn between an objective interest in public control of the land and an ideological interest that worships private property and distrusts public authority. In BC we have all benefitted from Crown lands and we should not let that commonwealth be dismembered. Hardly a week passes without some greedy interest making a claim for this jointly-held land, and as four-wheelers we must fight against this.

The behaviour of corporations is crucial to the future of four-wheeling. Companies hire skilled technicians to devise plans for the extraction of timber, but very little thought goes into the post-harvest use of logging roads. A typical example is the main line logging road, built so close to a beautiful lake shore that it will be forever impossible to add campsites. The needs of campers, hikers and four-wheelers should be taken into consideration before logging so that, during the forty years between harvests, the pleasure of others is possible. I know of dozens of places where a hundred yards of trail, from the end of the slash to a pond or pass or vista, would transform a rather dreary logging road into an attractive recreation spot. Some forest roads should cross from one valley to the next, allowing four-wheelers and backpackers to travel more easily through our backcountry. Good corporate citizenship should be encouraged in the forest industry.

Some firms are relatively open to recreational use of their timber licensed land, others are not. Those who keep

Trucks gathered for the night, after a long day

the gates closed only add to the burden of the others. Logging company employees should be trained to provide accurate advice and assistance to recreational users. Placing information and warning signs should also be considered a duty.

Multiple use of land is inevitable in most cases. Harmonizing the diverse interests of industry, government and the public will require considerable creativity and co-operation. Four-wheeling groups should be given appropriate status for consulting and advising on government policies affecting land use.

While four-wheelers have the prime responsibility for increased public understanding of off-roading, it would be extremely nice if other outdoor recreational organizations made an effort to understand our concerns. In the long run, we have more in common than we have need for disagreement, and the end of prejudices would be to our common advantage.

Four-wheeling has a great future and there is no better place to prove this than British Columbia. All who ride the backroads can contribute to this future.

SUGGESTED READING AND MAPS

GUIDEBOOKS

Bruce Fairley. *A Guide to Climbing & Hiking in Southwestern British Columbia*. Vancouver: Gordon Soules, 1986.

This remains a standard guide for climbers. Some of the terrain has changed, but it is still useful.

Mary and David Macaree, *103 Hikes in Southwestern BC* (4th ed.). Vancouver: Douglas & McIntyre, 1994.

May of the trails described in this guide start at the end of old logging roads; some of them are 4WD roads.

MAPS

British Columbia Recreational Atlas, Ministry of Environment/Infomapp, 3rd ed. 1989.

This collection of maps covers the entire province at 1 cm = 6 km. Some of the more obscure trails are not shown, but the book is extremely useful for general orientation.

Outdoor Recreation Maps. Published by ITMB Publishing on behalf of the Outdoor Recreation Council of BC.

Selected maps cover most of the territory of southwestern BC at a 1:100,000 scale.

Ministry of Forests, *Recreation maps.* These maps may be obtained from local Forestry offices. They show forestry roads and campsites. 1 cm = 2.5 km.

Provincial Ministry of Environment topographical maps in the 1:100,000 and 1:125,000 series are always handy, even if often far outdated.

SOURCES OF BOOKS AND MAPS

Most bookstores and outdoor sporting goods stores carry both maps and books. World Wide Books and Maps in Vancouver, and Nixon's Maps and Charts in Langley are good sources.